SOCIALISM
Dream and Reality

Brian Crozier

The Sherwood Press

First published 1987

© Brian Crozier 1987

The Sherwood Press Ltd, 88 Tylney Road, London E7 0LY

ISBN 0 907671 29 2

Typeset in Times by BookEns, Saffron Walden
Printed and bound by Redwood Burn Ltd, Trowbridge, Wiltshire

Contents

Prehistory

This book has a short prehistory, which I shall explain to avoid possible confusion. The chapters that constitute Book Three of the present volume originally appeared in *Socialism Explained* (Sherwood Press, 1984), of which I was a co-author with Arthur Seldon, and with cartoons by Cummings.

I originally wrote Books One and Two ('The Dreamers' and 'The Doers') in French for a proposed Paris edition which has not yet materialised, translating my French into English as I went along.

With revisions by both authors, and still with Cummings's cartoons, the enlarged book was published in New York in late 1986, under the title: *Socialism — The Grand Delusion* (Universe Books).

The present version, much revised and brought up to date, consists only of my own chapters. The reasons for the new formula are simple but need to be stated. Our original intention was satirical as well as serious. The book was respectful of the facts, but the tone was polemical.

It seemed to me, however, that there was a need for a readable but less light-hearted and more enduring approach to the subject. I therefore decided to write the new chapters, which in effect constitute a highly condensed history of socialist thought in the nineteenth and early twentieth centuries, with a comparative survey of socialist experiments in the Soviet Union under Lenin, in Nazi Germany and in Fascist Italy, as well as in Western Europe. The original chapters covering the USSR, Eastern Europe, the Far East and the Third World, and the advanced countries of the West, have been brought up to date.

This new and more sober survey omits the Cummings cartoons, some of which, in any case, had been overtaken by events; and (with the amicable consent of my co-author) the chapters by Arthur Seldon.

B. C.

PROLOGUE:
The Dream

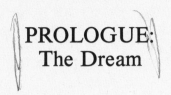

In the marketplace of political and economic options socialism is always on offer, no matter how many and how disappointing its failures in practice. In the communist countries, indeed, it is the only option. As the arch-capitalist Henry Ford used to say, his customers could have a car any colour they chose—so long as it was black.

The persistence of the socialist option, in the face of its evident failure, is a curious phenomenon. As Pope put it: 'Hope springs eternal in the human breast.' Too often, though, his next line is forgotten: 'Man never Is, but always To be blest.'

A fair working assumption is that it is possible that socialism appeals to certain fundamental human aspirations or sentiments, some less noble than others: the desire for fairness and justice for all; the hope that basic needs may be catered for, without too much exertion; and, not least, envy of those richer than oneself, whether or not their wealth is the outcome of their endeavours.

With such philosophical questions, I am only marginally concerned in this wide-ranging, but necessarily incomplete, survey. My purpose is to summarise what socialists have offered over the last couple of centuries, and what has actually been delivered in the name of socialism. It begins with the philosophers—the dreamers—and continues with the politicians—the doers. My examples are drawn from many countries and from different periods, so that it cannot in fairness be claimed that I have concentrated only on cases that prove my contention that the failure of socialism is universal, varying only in degree. On the contrary, it is the contention itself that emerges as the only possible conclusion from the many examples studied.

THE 'GOLDEN AGE'

The early socialists looked back to a golden age that had never existed, except as myth. They were, understandably, appalled by the painfully visible hardships of the first Industrial Revolution. Surely the idyllic condition they saw as the Golden Age could not be lost forever? The miseries of the new urban poor, ill-fed, overworked, unquestionably exploited for the greater wealth of the new industrial masters, were intolerable. They sought the answer in socialism, in the creation of wealth in common and its distribution in the form of equal, or at least equitable, shares for all.

But the golden age of their idealised memories had never been. Famine and plague had reigned, recurring with dismal frequency and persistence. The great famine of the early fourteenth century had devastated much of Europe. The Napoleonic Wars had brought hunger in their train. Rioters crying for bread had run wild in Hyde Park in the 1860s, to the intense disturbance of Matthew Arnold. Earlier and in another clime, there were the bread riots of Milan in 1628, recalled by Alessandro Manzoni in his powerful novel, *I promessi sposi* (*The Betrothed*). Nor should we forget the terrible Irish famine of the 1840s, which stimulated the great migratory waves to America, Australia and elsewhere. Even in France, with its wonderfully fertile soil, famine was a recurring affliction through the centuries.

Socialism, then, was going to be the answer to such historically recorded disasters, whether there had ever been a Golden Age or not, and to the contemporary ills of industrialisation. Primitive societies, too, often, had had no choice but to consume the seedcorn, paying the inevitable penalty of famine and death. The wars of kings and nobles had forced starvation, and at times wild inflation, on the humble people.

Socialism would end all that. The capitalists were cornering the wealth created by the workers to invest in their own future and selfish prosperity. Depending on the philosopher, either groups or communes, or the State, would do the investing, for the benefit of the people.

ASPECTS OF A DREAM

Socialism was not exactly new in the nineteenth century, for the ancient philosophers had already thought of it. However, I am not concerned here with the ideas of Plato, nor of Sir Thomas More, or of the Italian Tommaso Campanella who, in *La città del sole* (*The City of the Sun*, 1602) advocated a form of communism. Not that the socialist ideas of the thinkers and dreamers of antiquity, of the Renaissance or of the seventeenth century are in themselves uninteresting; but they did not bring any lasting consequences.

The same cannot be said of the socialist philosophers of the nineteenth century, whose works left an indelible stamp—so that we are still suffering from the consequences of their dreams. For it would be wrong to think that the so-called 'Utopian' socialists—such as Robert Owen, the Count of Saint-Simon or Charles Fourier—were not influential. Karl Marx did his best to sweep them out of history by vilifying them, but he too was profoundly in their intellectual debt. Indeed, Marxian communism is but socialism to the *n*th degree, a Utopia Lenin achieved by clubbing those who resisted it or sending them to the Gulag.

To grasp what socialism means, in all its variety of forms, we must go back to its common source, that is, the ideas of Britain's Robert Owen and of France's Claude-Henri de Saint-Simon.

Although, on this point, historians have never been in absolute agreement, the word 'socialist' does occur more than once in 1826 and 1827 in the publication of the followers of Owen, the *Cooperative Magazine*. In France *Le Globe* used it in 1832 to describe the 'socialist' disciples of the Count of Saint-Simon. Thereafter, the *idea* of socialism spread very fast.

We shall dwell, though not in this Prologue, on the factional quarrels in Europe, on Fourier and Cabet, without forgetting the anarchism of Proudhon and the populism of Blanqui. The Chartists of England will find their place, as well as the Workers' Party of Jules Guesde. We shall not neglect Karl Marx and his generous friend Engels, nor the 'revisionists' in Germany. The Paris Commune will have its mention, as will the French socialist leader Jaurès. The creation of social democratic parties in various European countries will play its part in our story, as well as the 'Internationals'. Fabianism in Britain, Syndicalism in France: these two are part of the history of socialism, and the list is far from complete. Finally, no list of 'dreamers' would be complete without the great 'action dreamer', Lenin himself.

In our time especially, socialist ideas have proliferated. From social democracy, European style, to the totalitarian socialisms of Nazism and Fascism as well as of Soviet communism; to 'Arab', 'Burmese', 'African', 'Third World' and all the other varieties of contemporary socialism. There is no shortage of examples. Indeed, the definitions tend to get mixed up and confused, for there is no shortage of contradictions either.

As for achievements, incoherence reigns: the 'fundamentalists' of socialism assert, without a smile, that 'true' socialism has never been achieved anywhere. This almost comes down to saying that socialism is not merely a dream, it is also a *mirage*. The closer one draws to it, the farther away it seems. The dreamers of socialism need a good supply of courage, or of imagination, or of simple naïveté to stay the course.

Robert Owen, the capitalist converted to his own idea of a communal socialism, could at least offer himself the luxury of an experiment in microcosm with his 'model' communities in America and elsewhere— all of them, of course, destined to go bankrupt. Saint-Simon, on his side, had offered himself the mystical satisfaction of a possible union between religion and social philosophy. As far as Marx was concerned, all that was socialism for laughs. In fact, it was not until our twentieth century that the real *practice* of socialism made its debut. In Russia especially, with the fanaticised socialism of Lenin and the monstrous cruelty of Stalin; in Germany and in Italy; and after World War II, in the universe of the peoples' democracies in Eastern Europe, China and elsewhere.

In Western Europe a kind of socialism took root in Sweden, where capitalists are not liquidated but merely bled, the better to extract the wealth they have created; in Austria, where a distinctive form of 'socialism' (which some observers say is no such thing) has had its successes. Among the great Western democracies, France had the unhappy experience of the Popular Front of Léon Blum, and more recently lived through the curious experiment of President Mitterrand, to which we shall return. In Spain, Republican socialism did not survive the victory of the Nationalist forces in the Civil War, although Franco himself practised his own brand of socialism between 1939 and 1957. In Britain, a 'right-wing' socialist government ('right-wing' in the sense that it was deeply anti-communist) in power between 1945 and 1951 created a semi-socialist State by wholesale nationalisation and the introduction of an advanced system of social security. Even in the United States, the 'citadel' of capitalism, a form of socialism, introduced through Roosevelt's New Deal, still exists but in a scattered way, given the Federal Constitution of that vast country.

In this Third World, systems claiming to be 'socialist' established themselves in India, in Burma, in Egypt (at least in principle), in Ghana, in Tanzania, pending the advent of 'Marxist' regimes in the former Portuguese colonies of Angola and Mozambique, and in Zimbabwe, as Southern Rhodesia decided to call itself. If one adds Cuba, Vietnam and North Korea to the list (which even then is incomplete) it is fair to say that in our own period there is no shortage of socialist experiments. It is therefore relatively easier than ever before to study socialism as a phenomenon, and, above all, to make what seems to me to be a necessary comparison between the dream and the reality, between plans and achievements.

Everywhere, I repeat, the results have been disappointing. In the USSR the economy appears to be permanently bogged down, and more and more dependent on the (suicidal?) benefactions of the West and of Japan. In China the disastrous experiments of Mao Zedong caused one of his successors, Deng Xiaoping, to initiate 'capitalist' experiments in certain regions, with quite astonishing results. In the Far East, incidentally, capitalism has taken off whenever it has been allowed to practise: in Japan, in South Korea, in Hong Kong, in Taiwan the achievements have been spectacular and offer a truly striking contrast with the poverty created by socialist regimes.

In Britain, socialist ideas, which Conservative governments did little to resist before the advent of Mrs Thatcher in 1979, have virtually ruined what had been a flourishing economy. In Federal Germany one notes a distinct impoverishment during the period in power of the Social Democrats (SPD) from 1969 onwards. In France it took the socialists (initially in power with the communists) a mere year or two at the most to undo the prosperity achieved by M. Mitterrand's predecessors. In Africa, the contrast between the socialised misery of Tanzania and the relative prosperity of Kenya has deeply impressed all travellers to both places.

Yet, to understate the point, this was not at all what the socialists, whether philosophers or politicians, told us to expect. Taking a bit from here and a bit from there, the socialist option includes some or all of the following checklist of promises or predictions:

(1) Common ownership would lead to greatly increased output.
(2) There would be a fairer, more even distribution of wealth. Instead of the rich getting richer while the poor got poorer, the poor would gradually be brought up to the level of the rich.
(3) Class conflicts would be eliminated. (The way Marx saw it, and Lenin did it, the physical elimination of the exploiting classes would make a giant contribution to the classless society.)
(4) All would participate equally in the political process. Did not Lenin say that 'every cook should learn to govern the country—participate in policy formation and decision taking'?
(5) No more economic fluctuations: the 'cyclical crises' of capitalism would end.
(6) Racial and cultural distinctions would be ironed out, as well as social classes.
(7) Wars would end when the world consisted of socialist States, because the instabilities of capitalism and conflicting interests between rival ruling classes would have vanished.

Ah, well . . .

THE UNIVERSAL RULES

In the hard reality, as distinct from the rosy dream, three Universal Rules of socialism emerge from this inquiry.

The first Universal Rule of socialism is that it fails wherever it is tried. It does not matter whether it calls itself Burmese socialism or African, whether the experiment takes place in Sweden or Tanzania or Cuba, it simply does not work.

The second Universal Rule is that the degree of failure is proportionate with the degree of socialism: the more there is of it, the worse the failure—allowing for other factors such as the stage of development reached before the experiment began and the aptitude for economic development of the nations and peoples concerned in the light of history, civilisation, culture, climate and any other relevant factor.

I hope in this second part of our study to demonstrate the truth of my first two Universal Rules.

There is, however, a third Universal Rule, no less important than the other two: socialism is incompatible with freedom. Here again, the degree to which socialism has been adopted or imposed is crucial. Anybody who doubts my third Universal Rule is invited to look at the plight of the people in the most extreme socialist regimes in the world, which are probably those of the Chinese People's Republic, North Korea and Vietnam. In all three, individual freedom has been virtually extinguished.

This was particularly true of China under Mao Zedong, although the myth of Mao as a great and farsighted leader was uncritically swallowed by many well-meaning people who would not have relished living under the tyranny he had established by force in his vast and ancient country. In all three of these Far Eastern 'models' of socialism, you cannot marry a person of your choice (as a Chinese girl discovered in the post-Mao period when she made the mistake of falling in love with a French diplomat). Nor can you change your job at will: the all-pervasive Party tells you where to work, and in China, in particular, the Party might decide that it would do an intellectual good to work in the fields in a distant province.

In such countries you cannot travel freely, either in the country or abroad. In North Korea, the Soviet-invented device of the 'internal passport' has become a thick book with a detailed family history back to the grandparents as a record of just about everything you have done and said in your life to date. As for travel abroad, only official visits are sanctioned, and then only in groups closely supervised by the secret police. As for emigrating, you do have the option of joining others in a leaky boat and risking your life on the high seas, as with the Vietnamese 'boat people'.

As for political rights, they are non-existent. Both China and Vietnam once experimented briefly with carefully metered political freedom in the 1950s. As Mao put it, 'Let one hundred flowers bloom, let one hundred schools of thought contend'. The North Vietnamese (as they then were) did much the same. In both countries, the degree of dissent revealed was so startling to the regimes that the lid was promptly clamped down again. Then after Mao Zedong had died, and the relatively pragmatic Deng Xiaoping had taken over, ordinary (that is, non-Party) people were allowed to write their opinions on a long slab of bricks in Peking known as 'Democracy Wall'. That, too, was a short-lived diversion.

But surely, some readers may say, you are talking about *communist*, not socialist, regimes. Should not a distinction be made between the two?

The short answer to this legitimate query is that, again, it is all a question of degree. All communist regimes are totalist* in that the ruling Communist Party (whether or not it uses the word 'Communist' in its designation: some do not) controls every aspect of people's lives, non-political as well as political. But not one of them, including the prototype model of all in the Soviet Union, claims to have achieved 'communism'. The promise of 'communism', seen as the advent of abundance for all, is like a mirage, ever receding into the distance, always in the future. The most these regimes claim is that they have achieved 'socialism', or that they are 'building' it. The Soviets claim to have *built* it, and to be pushing on towards communism, to be achieved at some unspecified date in the (far) future.

Indeed, the Soviets refer to their East European empire (which is what it is) as the 'Socialist Commonwealth'; not, say, as the 'communist bloc'. To describe the existing communist regimes as 'socialist' is thus merely to take them at their own valuation. The point is that socialism has been taken further in the communist countries than elsewhere, and it must be assumed that this is because it takes a totalist, one-party State to impose full socialism. Which merely illustrates the proposition that socialism extinguishes freedom.

In party democracies, where political parties may alternate in power or need to form coalitions to survive in office, there is at least a glimmer

---

* The word 'totalitarian' is said to have been coined by Mussolini's adviser Giovanni Gentile, who used it in a speech on 8 March 1925. Five years later, Mussolini referred to 'the totalitarian State.' The neologism thereafter passed into the language—indeed into all languages. This fact apparently conferred upon it a kind of sacrosanct aura. For my taste, 'totalitarian' and 'totalitarianism' are heavy and inelegant. I propose to substitute briefer forms with identical meanings: 'totalist' and 'totalism'.

of hope, in that a new coalition or the advent of an anti-socialist party to power, may be given a chance to undo some, at least, of the harm done by the previous government's socialist programme.

Even in party democracies, however, the advance of socialism can be insidious, to the point where it is hard to reverse. As the late Georges Albertini put it, 'Socialism is communism in homoeopathic doses.' In recent years Britain's Labour Party has called for 'a fundamental and irreversible shift in the balance of power and wealth in favour of working people and their families'. If this aim is ever achieved—that is, if 'irreversible' socialism is introduced—then indeed the liberties of the British people will have been extinguished.

In Western countries, until very recently, incoming non-socialist governments have been content on the whole to administer the situation they have inherited, whatever the degree of socialism their predecessors may have introduced. To that extent the march of socialism has tended to be 'irreversible'. In 1979 and 1980, however, two Western leaders committed to reversing the irreversible were elected to high office: Mrs Margaret Thatcher and President Ronald Reagan. Each has aimed at reducing the State's share of the national cake. In other words, at reducing the degree of socialism achieved by outgoing administrations. It is too early to judge to what extent these efforts will prove successful. That they are necessary and deserve full support, I do not doubt. In Britain, especially, the inroads of socialism had seriously undermined the freedom of the individual in recent years.

In France, the conservative (or, as the French say, 'liberal') prime minister, Jacques Chirac, was faced with the paradoxical task of undoing the damage caused by the preceding Socialist administration while the Socialist President, François Mitterrand, remained in supreme office.

The case of Swedish socialism is of particular interest, and I shall give it close attention later on. Unlike other socialist-inclined countries, the emphasis in Sweden has not been on the nationalisation (or socialisation) of the means of production, distribution and exchange (to quote from the notorious Clause IV of the Constitution of Britain's Labour Party). By and large, industry has been left in private hands, to create wealth which the State can then expropriate in the furtherance of socialism. (The party that has ruled Sweden for all but six years during the past five decades calls itself Social Democratic, but its former leader, the late Olof Palme, was ideologically closer to the Soviets than to the Americans.)

The accumulated outcome of socialist policies in Sweden has been a regime which has the outer trappings of democracy—political parties, an elected parliament, a theoretically free press—but in which the prevailing socialist consensus has so far reduced individual freedom as to cause a British writer (Roland Huntford, who served in Stockholm as correspondent of the London *Observer*) to describe the Swedes as 'The New Totalitarians' (the title of the book he wrote about socialist Sweden). Once again, socialism and freedom are shown to be incompatible.

I have made only passing reference, so far, to the Union of Soviet Socialist Republics, but as the longest continuous experiment in socialism (1917 to 1987, so far), the Soviet Union is clearly of the utmost importance. There is a paradox here.

The Soviet Union is one of the most repressive regimes in the world, but it is *less totalist* than the regimes of China, North Korea and Vietnam in that it is marginally but significantly easier for ordinary people to opt out of the political process in the USSR than in the three Far Eastern socialist regimes. In China, for instance, every street, every small village has its Party committee, bullying or cajoling ordinary people to do the Party's bidding; although life became much easier after Mao had died. In the USSR, no dissent is tolerated, but the Party is less all-pervasive. Corruption is rampant and the black market is a way of life: indeed it is hardly an exaggeration to say that it keeps the economic system alive by preventing it from choking on the socialism of centralised planning. True, those on the fiddle, who perform a useful function, put themselves permanently at risk. Some 'economic crimes' are punishable by death. But to the extent that the fiddlers and black marketeers defeat the paralysis inherent in socialism, they contribute a tiny ray of freedom in the surrounding blackness.

Unfortunately for non-socialists and freedom-lovers, the demonstration of the generalised bankruptcy of socialism may not be enough. For fundamentalists, 'true' socialism does not exist anywhere. Real-life experiences do not count. Socialism is always something to be built in the future.

In the eyes of the communists socialism has already been created in the Soviet Union, but its survival (and therefore, in the last analysis, its permanent success) can be ensured only if 'capitalism' (that is, pluralist democracy and the market economy) is destroyed throughout the world. By then it will be rather late.

In our Western countries the voters are in general better provided with common sense than the theoreticians. It is the electorate, finally, that will take note of the generalised bankruptcy of socialism and will organise the funeral of 'the Grand Delusion'.

BOOK ONE

The Dreamers

1

First of the Many

ROBERT OWEN

A gentle, charming, delightful fellow. Everybody seems to agree that Robert Owen was that kind of man, and he had many friends. Later on, when he reached the point of believing in the absolute truth of his own ideas, the comment tended to be: 'A gentle bore.' That, at any rate, was the way the great historian Thomas Babington Macaulay put it. As soon as Owen started speaking, he would try to run away.

Born in 1771, Owen grew up when the Industrial Revolution was at its height. He was deeply affected by the long war between England and Napoleonic France, by labour agitation, by the economic crisis which followed the peace of 1815, and by the parliamentary reform movement.

Born in Wales (as one would expect with his name), he left his native village aged nine in search of fortune and adventure. At eighteen he borrowed £100, which became his capital. He bought one of the new weaving machines and, with remarkable speed, became a leading manufacturer at New Lanark in Scotland. A natural philanthropist, he turned it into a model factory where the workers enjoyed pay and conditions that were quite exceptional at that time—which shortly preceded the 'social' novels of Charles Dickens.

His business partners used to complain to him about such misplaced generosity. What interested *them* was profits. For Owen, however, the profit motive was of little interest, although his factory always did pretty well, since he was an excellent manager. As for the profits, he dipped into them, at first so that he could improve working conditions and later to finance his social experiments, one of which was the building of special schools to improve the future prospects of the sons and daughters of his workforce. His partners raised more and more objections and managed to get rid of him in 1809. He stepped down, but not for long. At that time, he had a number of rich Quaker friends, and some

3

of them readily agreed to become his new partners. In 1813 they bought back New Lanark for him, and he made a triumphant return.

He had started to write the previous year. Already, he had declared intellectual war on capitalism, for he was in no sense a violent revolutionary. He liked to reason and to persuade. Indeed, that was how he became a 'bore' and his friends began to find him tedious company. He clashed with the Church of England, rejecting the doctrine of Man's personal responsibility. As far as Owen was concerned, it was the environment that determined character. All you need do is to reform the environment, he used to say, and you will reform characters. This was the message of his first major work, *A New View of Society: Essays on the Principle of the Formation of Character*. But by far the most important of Robert Owen's works was undoubtedly his *Report to the County of Lanark* (published in Glasgow in 1821). Here was the first full-length expression of his idea of socialism.

By then, Owen's ambitions extended well beyond his personal micro-cosm. He wanted to extend its principles, first to the whole of Britain and thereafter to all humanity. One of Karl Marx's key ideas was first expressed by Owen in this sentence: 'Manual work, well directed, is the source of all wealth and of national prosperity.' The good citizens of Lanark did not quite know what to make of it. Of course they were impressed by the concrete side of Owen's enterprise, but found his idealism harder to digest.

Owen was always ready to convert his dream into reality. He launched his 'communities', which he called 'villages of co-operation'. He had no self-doubts. He was quite sure he could demonstrate through his workers' communities that it is possible to abolish the sterile distinctions caused by the division of labour, to reform the currency of basing it on the intrinsic value of the work accomplished, and to share all goods equally. This was the true start of Owenism, or British socialism, and indeed the terms became virtually interchangeable. The workers followed him with enthusiasm, the political class not at all. He was accused of wanting to create 'communities of paupers'.

Between 1824 and 1829 Robert Owen spent most of his time in America. He was very attracted to this new society, and what interested him was that it was less set in its ways, less weighed down by the heritage of the conventions of an older society. There, he thought, was the fertile ground he was looking for to create his *brand* of socialism. In 1825 he bought a property of more than 5,000 acres, named 'Harmony', which had belonged to a German religious community known as the Rappites. Situated on the banks of the River Wabash in Indiana, it consisted of a well-constructed village and silk and woollen workshops. The ground was fertile and there were rich pastures and productive orchards.

The whole complex seemed most propitious for the needs of our reformer–philosopher. The Germans at Harmony had lived a frugal life which was prosperous within its limits. To mark his take-over Owen put an adjective in front of the name. His new model community would henceforth be known as 'New Harmony'.

He announced the launch of his social experiment with as much publicity as he could muster. He invited volunteers to participate, and soon they were flocking in. Indeed, there were too many of them, which led to an immediate housing shortage. Since the idea of careful selection does not seem to have occurred to him, there was a plethora of idealists, each of whom had his or her own idea of what a socialist community ought to be; and a shortage of skilled workers, especially carpenters. Despite all his efforts, the community broke down within a couple of years. Disappointed, but in no way discouraged, Robert Owen came home.

His philosophy now took on new dimensions. 'His' socialism was turned into a new system of morals, almost a religion. In this way, too, he anticipated Marx, who, of course, considered religion in the normal sense as 'the opium of the people'. He brought out *The Book of the New Moral World*, which became the Bible of his disciples, now more and more numerous. He went further and attacked marriage as a religious institution. Instead, he proposed a civil form of union between men and women, bound by an easily dissoluble contract.

During Owen's absence in America his disciples had started a number of communities on the Owenite model. All of them went broke. He himself launched two new ones, which also broke down. Between times, the workers' movement had grown significantly, and the first trades unions had been set up, despite a campaign in Parliament to make them illegal.

On his side, Owen now founded a gigantic organisation which he called the 'Great Consolidated Trades Union', to rally what he called the 'productive classes'. Two years later, towards the end of 1834, his 'trades union' broke down in its turn. In their thousands, his disciples deserted him. By then, Robert Owen was 63. Disappointed by his successful failures, but in no way shaken in his convictions, he dropped action in favour of words. He would go on to write ten more books, and to give a good many lectures.

A lonely old man, Robert Owen lived on until 1858, and died aged 87. For some time before his death he had been finding consolation in the new vogue of spiritualism. Despite the failures, despite the rejection of his ideas during his lifetime, Owenism survived him. Indeed, it became the basis of the co-operative and labour movement in Britain.

SAINT-SIMON AND THE SAINT-SIMONIANS

Claude-Henri de Rouvroy, Count of Saint-Simon, was about ten years older than Robert Owen, but since he did not begin his career as a writer until he was 42, they may be considered contemporaries as far as intellectual activity was concerned.

Born in 1760, Saint-Simon was deeply affected by the French Revolution, which he had witnessed as a young man. He claimed direct descent from the Emperor Charlemagne, and belonged to the same family as the more famous Duke of Saint-Simon, the chronicler of the reign of Louis XIV. Wide-ranging curiosity was a main characteristic of this freedom-loving aristocrat. He had fought in Lafayette's army in America, which meant that he had lived through a first revolution, the American one, before witnessing a second—the French Revolution. He had a rather special view of great historical upheavals, and he had noted that the revolution in religious and philosophical thought led respectively by Luther and Descartes had happened *after* the collapse of the medieval system; that Newton had made his great discoveries *after* the English Civil War; and that the ideas of the philosopher Locke had *followed* the 'Glorious Revolution' of 1688. He therefore confidently expected that a new revolution, a 'scientific' one, would take place before long in France. Moreover, he was deeply convinced that it would fall to him, Saint-Simon, to be its leading spirit.

In his view a new era was about to begin: the era of science and scientists. To be fair to him, in some respects Saint-Simon was anticipating the advent of the technocrats of the twentieth century rather than of the men of science of the nineteenth. Man, he thought, must master his environment. His admiration for the great scientists of his age, particularly d'Alembert and Condorcet, was boundless. He envisaged a scientific revolution to be led by men of this calibre.

Saint-Simon had spent some time in Mexico, where he had gone after his American battles. There he had proposed to the Emperor the construction of a canal to link the Atlantic and Pacific Oceans. Back in Europe, he visited Spain, where he proposed the building of a canal to link Madrid with the sea. These ideas came to nothing at the time. The Revolution broke out in France, and Saint-Simon came home. He put the prevailing disorder to good use and made a fortune by speculating on the market. His excuse was that he needed money to extend his range of knowledge and of the varied experience he felt he needed to acquire. Ironically, the money did not last very long, and Saint-Simon spent much of his adult life in poverty.

Napoleon was already the master of France when Saint-Simon began his career as a writer and philosopher, and his first titles are highly suggestive. They include *Introductions to the Scientific Works of the Nineteenth Century* (1802), *Sketch for a New Encyclopaedia* (1810) and *A Memoir on Universal Gravity* (1813)—at first glance, hardly the reflections of a political thinker.

In fact, Saint-Simon was appealing to the scientists of his time to create a 'science of humanity', a kind of gigantic synthesis of human knowledge, in which his new 'science of morals' would have a leading place. He wrote to Napoleon, whom he greatly admired, to appeal to him to set up a new 'universal academy'. But the Emperor turned a deaf ear.

Gradually, Saint-Simon became aware of the need for a political framework for his dominant idea of a scientific and moral revolution, but he seemed reluctant to go into specifics. What he wanted above all were order and peace, or peace in order. In collaboration with the historian Augustin Thierry he wrote a treatise, *Of the Reorganisation of European Society* (1814), proposing a plan for a European federation on the basis of an alliance between France and Britain—France for the great ideas, Britain for the organisation of industry to serve the betterment of the human condition.

In this first phase Saint-Simon's thoughts excluded religion. Towards the end of his life, however, he changed direction. In his view, the dogmas of the Church were, of course, out of date. But *sentiments*, morality and faith in the future of humanity would require a church of a new type. In his last work, *The New Christianity*, which remained unfinished, he proposed the creation of a new universal Church, a main function of which would be the control of education. This Church would be, so to speak, the concrete expression of a new religion based on science.

Was Saint-Simon really a socialist? In some respects he seems a long way both from his contemporary Robert Owen and from the socialist thinkers of the next generation, headed by Karl Marx. The class struggle, as the Marxists conceived it, was foreign to his way of thinking. There was indeed an element of the class struggle in Saint-Simon's thinking but he saw it in a completely different way from Marx. Where Marx called for a revolution of the workers against their 'capitalist oppressors', Saint-Simon envisaged the unity of the productive classes (industrialists, bankers and workers). On the other hand, he hated what he called the *idle* class (*la classe des oisifs*), by which he meant the old nobility (to which he himself belonged by birth) and the new, created by Napoleon.

In his model society the administration of the State would be in the hands of the industrialists and bankers, advised by the scientists. The exploitation of what he called 'the most numerous and poorest class' would cease by a natural process, for the unity of all the producers (both bosses and workers)—without, of course, any participation by the idle class—would be created on the basis of his new morality.

Saint-Simon had little time for individual freedoms, and the notion of democracy was entirely foreign to him. The Saint-Simonian universe was authoritarian, centralised and *dirigiste*. All this amounted to a technocracy before its time. Despite the gulf that separated him from the Marxists, he anticipated Marx's thought by his insistence on the dominant role of economic forces in the future evolution of society.

As far as we know, the word 'socialism' was not part of the Count of Saint-Simon's vocabulary, although his disciples were to use it. But that is hardly the question. Saint-Simon certainly was a socialist in certain respects—by his 'universalism', his authoritarian approach, his *dirigisme*, his idealism and his profound misunderstanding of human nature. In combination, these elements constituted a kind of guarantee of some future totalism. To establish peace and harmony between human beings in the future society he envisaged, all that would be necessary would be to put everybody to work to create a common prosperity. By adding a 'scientific' and universal Church, he anticipated—without being aware of it—the 'counter-church' of communist parties in power and the scientific pretensions of Karl Marx. Finally, with his 'new Christianity' he fell into a kind of messianism which was not all that distant (despite the spiritual element in it) from Leninism.

Saint-Simon's thinking, as reinterpreted by his disciples, rapidly became almost unrecognisable. Two personalities dominated the Saint-Simonian movement: Barthélemy-Prosper Enfantin, who became its natural leader, and Saint-Amand Bazard, who undertook the difficult task of extracting the essential elements of the master's thinking, extrapolating from them wherever necessary and turning them into a coherent doctrine. The first of these created a church, without either Pope or cardinals but with a 'Father' and 'Apostles'. The other was editorially responsible for a work produced in common, *The Saint-Simonian Doctrine* (1826–8). In substance, Saint-Simonism turned into a form of State socialism. It called for the abolition of the inheritance of private property, which in effect implied that henceforth the State would be the sole heir of inherited property instead of the sons of a family. This would enable the State to create a central fund which would constitute a kind of capital reserve, to be distributed thereafter to those enterprises best fitted to make good use of it by means of an enormous central bank.

As for the Saint-Simonian church, as with many sects, it is perhaps hard to take it seriously, with its internal schisms and its universal pretensions. Accused of having plotted against the State, Enfantin spent a year in prison. Later he would play a role in the building of the railway linking Paris to the Mediterranean via Lyon, and in planning the Suez Canal project in which he saw the practical expression of the religion of work the master had advocated.

We need not spend too much time on such fantasies. In Saint-Simonism the absurd quite often rubbed shoulders with the sublime. For good and for bad, Saint-Simon's thinking made a profound mark on its era.

FOURIER, CABET AND SOME OTHERS

Between Saint-Simon and his compatriot and contemporary, François-Marie-Charles Fourier, there was a virtually total contrast. Saint-Simon reasoned in universal terms; Fourier in microcosm. Saint-Simon (like our own Owen) underestimated the importance of human nature by subordinating it to the environment; Fourier boasted that he had made an exhaustive study of human nature and that he had thought through his proposed remoulding of society in the light of his analysis.

Born at Besançon of a middle-class family that had been virtually ruined by the Revolution, Fourier had to earn his living as a clerk and travelling salesman. Whatever leisure he could find was spent in writing books. Other writers had very little influence on him. He had reached on his own the conclusion which, at any rate at first sight, seemed full of good sense. Since human nature is diverse, and human beings are easily bored, it seemed to him essential to create a new type of community where all possible characters would find their place, where each would do the work that suited him or her best and where, therefore, nobody need be bored.

The obvious question was: 'Who's going to do the dirty jobs?' His answer was ready-made: the children. He was not joking. Children, he argued, actually like to get dirty when playing. Through an appropriate system of education they would be taught to transform their games into constructive work. He envisaged the creation of model communities in some respects not unlike those of Robert Owen but much more highly structured. Each of his communities (which he named *phalanstères*, from the Greek *phalanx*) would consist of all the types of character he had analysed. Limited in number to 1,600 or 1,800—with, of course, equal numbers of men and women—the *phalanstères* would concentrate on agricultural output, and their members would change jobs whenever they wished and on condition that the exchange was agreeable to others concerned.

Whereas Saint-Simon was frankly authoritarian and *dirigiste*, Fourier wanted to do everything on the voluntary principle. The produce of the *phalanstères* would be distributed in proportions decided in advance, with one share for the workers, another for the capital reserve and a final portion to be set aside to recompense such members as had shown exceptional initiative or talent.

Once the principle had been established Fourier launched an appeal for capital and for the volunteers he needed. For years, it seems, he lunched alone in a restaurant he had named as a meeting-place, waiting for the capital and volunteers, which never seemed to come. It was only after his death, in 1837, that *phalanstères* were created, especially in America but also in Russia, Spain and Romania. None of them lasted very long. In fact, most of the volunteers he had waited for in vain in his restaurant but who had attempted the adventure of creating the *phalanstères* after his death were, almost by definition, intellectuals and without any marked aptitude for hard work in the fields.

Fourier had carried his analysis of characters into the sexual domain, as witness the following passage quoted by his biographer Emile Lehouck:[1]

> I was leaving a large city, where apparently cuckoldry had not gone out of fashion, for I had drawn up my list of 72 kinds of cuckolds, each distinct from the others . . .

He had even drawn up a synoptic table of his cuckolds. He was a bachelor and had developed a taste for orgies in which he took part, particularly during his trips to Lyon, and foresaw the introduction of orgies in the behavioural pattern of his future 'Harmony'. His treatise, *The New World of Love*, contains many deliciously unexpected passages.

As death approached, Fourier went mad. This is perhaps not surprising. In principle he had been sensible enough to make allowances for human nature. But in practice he had not grasped that reliance on volunteers virtually guaranteed the failure of his communal experiments. The posthumous demonstration of this reality is not without importance. Only coercion would have guaranteed the survival of his model communities, which practically comes down to saying that in the last analysis socialist ideas 'work' only under constraint.

Fourier's influence turned out to be a good deal weaker than Saint-Simon's. Having said that, Marx undoubtedly owed him the principle of the limitation of production to the mere satisfaction of needs. Fourier was against the 'superfluous' abundance of capitalism. Present-day socialists also owe him the principle of full employment, the application of which has strongly contributed to the economic ruin of Britain in the post-war decades. The principles of 'progressive' education (that is, at the pleasure of the children) may also be charged to Charles Fourier's account.

Leaving Robert Owen aside, it is fair to say that in its origins at least, socialism is a *French idea*. I repeat, I am not aiming at writing an exhaustive treatise, but it would be wrong to leave out certain names, especially those of Cabet, Sismondi, Blanqui, Louis Blanc and Proudhon; that is, in the same order, Communist Utopia, *petit bourgeois* socialism (an expression coined by Marx and Engels), revolutionary violence, syndical (that is, trades union) organisation and anarchism. All these tendencies have in fact contributed to the curious whole we call socialism.

A lawyer by training, Etienne Cabet (1788–1856), as with so many others, served his apprenticeship as a revolutionary within the secret Italo-French society known as the Carbonari. He had taken part in the revolution of 1830. Appointed Prosecutor-General of Corsica, he was dismissed because of the radical attacks he was continually making against the policies of the 'bourgeois' monarchy. After some years in exile in England, where Robert Owen's ideas deeply impressed him, he came home soaked in extremist radicalism. Henceforth he preached the nationalisation of all means of production and communal life. Soon, he and his disciples were being called 'communists'.

Cabet is yet another writer of the period who wrote his own Utopia then tried to bring it to life. In 1840 he published his *Journey to Icaria*, an imaginary country where all citizens were equal, where private property had been abolished, where each contributed his or her labour on equal terms of the others. There was to be uniformity in dress (to avoid class distinction), equality of the sexes, and collective use of the means of production. Cabet wanted to preserve the family, and as an exception to his rule of sexual equality, as Orwell would have put it, some were going to be 'more equal than others', since the father (and never the mother) was to be recognised as the head of the family.

In 1848 a group of his disciples emigrated to Texas, there to found the Icaria of his dreams. He himself followed the next year with another group. Finally he created Icaria in Illinois. Alas, here as elsewhere, failure was on the way. Cabet had hoped to found a city of one million inhabitants, but the number never surpassed 1,500. Still, on this reduced scale, Icaria, to be succeeded by 'New Icaria', turned out to be more durable than the Utopias of Owen or Fourier. This one lasted until 1895, nearly 30 years after the death of its founder. Cabet was a believer. After the exultation of his youth, he became a pacifist. In his work *True Christianity*, he cited the 'communism' of the early Christians as the example to be followed.

Jean-Charles-Léonard-Simonde de Sismondi, a Genevan of French origin, was one of the most prolific authors of the nineteenth century.

His *History of the Italian Republics* filled 16 volumes, and his *History of the French*, 31. As a youth, he had lived in England. He went back there in 1818, after an absence of 24 years, and came home shocked by the misery of the proletariat, which he attributed without qualification to capitalism and to the *laissez-faire* of the 'classical' economists, Adam Smith and Ricardo. In his book, *New Principles Of Political Economy*, he denounced capitalism as the source of misery and unemployment, and called for State intervention to guarantee a worker a minimum salary and social security.

Like most of the socialists of his time, Sismondi became the target of bitter attacks by Karl Marx. This did not prevent the latter from borrowing his theory of 'underconsumption'. With Marx in tow, Sismondi was first to use the following argument. The purchasing power available to buy industrial products depends on the volume of capital in circulation used for the employment of labour. Another way of putting it would be that it depended on the size of the 'wages fund'. By keeping the level of wages as low as possible, at the subsistence level in fact, whereas capital funds used for investment in machine tools never ceased to rise, the capitalists were simultaneously increasing the industrial production of consumer goods. In consequence, the system could be maintained only by the liquidation in repeated crises of much of the capital over-invested in large-scale industry. This process, he reasoned, was bound to deepen still further the misery of the masses.

As for politics, Sismondi was against democracy and universal suffrage on the ground that neither the working class nor the lower middle class was conditioned for them. Was Sismondi a socialist? Probably not, in the full sense of the term. But what is certain is that he influenced the socialists in a significant way by his economic analyses.

Long before Lenin, Louis-Auguste Blanqui (1805–81) was the very model of a total revolutionary. When he died he had spent 33 of his 76 years in prison. There is no need to follow him in all his peripatetic adventures, his plots, his insurrections. Let us rather concentrate on his socialist ideas.

I note in passing, however, that, in common with Cabet and others, he had been a member of the secret society of the Carbonari and had taken part in the revolution of 1830. Later on he would found his own clandestine organisations, among them the Society of Families and the Society of Seasons. As for his thinking, one idea dominated his tumultuous life: the creation of a small revolutionary elite, which would be ready to seize power by force whenever it judged the circumstances to be right. In contrast to Marx, he did not see the need for a mass party. Once in power, his little group was to establish an interim dictatorship, to organise the workers and transform society. In effect, it was going to be revolution by improvisation.

Being a man of action above all, Blanqui left very few writings that were more than ephemeral. His ideas are to be found especially in articles which he wrote for various journals, notably in *Le Libérateur* and *La Patrie en Danger*. His biographer Maurice Dommanget[2] attributes to Blanqui a chapter of a work which he produced in collaboration with scientist Raspail and a law student named Antony Thouret, entitled *Au Peuple, Société des amis du Peuple* (To the People, Society of the Friends of the People), published in July 1831, exactly a year after the events of 1830.

In this chapter, which came out during one of his multiple stays in prison, Blanqui asserted that he was a socialist, and referred to the division of society, as he saw it, into two great social categories: on one side, 'the classes that were well off and opulent', the 'privileged class', 'the aristocracy'; on the other, 'the poor and ignorant masses', the 'people'. In his eyes these two categories were so clearly define that they almost constituted 'two very distinct races of men'. Henceforth Blanqui envisaged the triumph of the people over the privileged and the advent of a proletarian and socialist republic.

Later, in the first numbers of *Le Libérateur*, of which he was the editor, Blanqui sharpened up his ideas, notably in the following passage, quoted by Dommanget:

> Equality is our faith; we march with ardour and confidence under its holy banner, full of veneration and enthusiasm for the immortal defenders of that faith, animated by the same devotion as they, ready as they are to spill all our blood for its triumph.

Obviously, these are words of exaltation rather than of serious reflection.

Despite the failures, the treacheries, the years in prison, Blanqui's revolutionary faith never weakened. There is nothing unusual about that: that is the way fanatics are.

Taking advantage of the defeat of Napoleon III at Sedan he attempted with his followers to overthrow the government. This ended in yet another failure. Having taken refuge in the countryside, Blanqui was eventually arrested and found himself—yet again!—in gaol during the Paris Commune, in which his followers had played a part. During the last years of his life he started calling himself 'communist'. Despite the factional disputes between Blanquists and Marxists, Blanqui and Marx coincided on quite a number of points, notably on the need for a dictatorship of the proletariat and on the concept that the product of the workers was being 'stolen' from them by their capitalist oppressors.

Whereas Blanqui wanted a dictatorship to be set up by force, Louis Blanc (1811–82) dreamed of a socialism to be achieved by gentleness and persuasion. In contrast to Blanqui, Blanc had opposed the Communards. The difference between them is significant. Blanc had an unshakable faith in democracy and universal suffrage, which put him at a distance not only from Blanqui but also from the Saint-Simonians. In Britain as in France, he is rightly considered as the precursor of 'democratic socialism'.

Born in Spain, the son of a French exile and his Spanish wife, Louis Blanc turned to France at the time of the Restoration of the Bourbons and made a career as a lawyer and publicist (*Le bon Sens* and *La Revue du progrès*). He made his reputation, instantly, with his work *Organisation du travail*, where most of his ideas are to be found. A lengthy stay in England made him aware of the evils of contemporary capitalism, as indeed happened with Cabet and Sismondi.

His theory of history was very different from that of Karl Marx. The latter believed he had found the key of history in the interplay of economic forces; for Blanc that key was to be found in the domain of ideas. In his view socialism would be made in part by the intervention of the State in economic planning and through social welfare and in part (much as Fourier thought) by small autonomous organisations or co-operatives, which he termed 'rural workshops'. The famous slogan appropriated by the Communist parties is attributed to him: 'From each according to his ability, to each according to his needs.'

The great majority of theoreticians of socialism were themselves either of bourgeois or even of aristocratic origin. In any case, they had been brought up in easy circumstances. The pity they felt for less-favoured classes was certainly sincere, and should in no way be held against them. The complementary phenomenon, which was the guilt complex of the middle classes, was far more controversial. Is one guilty for having been born in a well-off family? And it has to be said that the capitalists of the first period, especially in Britain during the Industrial Revolution did seem—certainly the majority of them—singularly indifferent to the miseries of their workforce.

It is only much later, during the period of the great Henry Ford of motor-car fame, that capitalists began to understand that it was in their own interests to increase wages and therefore purchasing power, leading to a broader market. Perhaps they should have thought of this earlier, but at the time of Louis Blanc and of Karl Marx, the 'conventional wisdom' (as John Kenneth Galbraith would have put it) was that the lower the wages, the higher the profits. It was exactly as though the capitalists were doing their best to prove the socialists right!

There was, however, an exception to the rule of well-off family circumstance: Pierre-Joseph Proudhon (1809–65). To borrow a phrase of Saint-Simon's, he came from the ranks of 'the most numerous and the poorest class'. He was the son of a country artisan and a peasant woman, and was born near Besançon. He remained proud of his humble origins. A self-taught man, he served an apprenticeship in a printing works, which gave him easy access to many books and made him a man of considerable erudition.

In the scale of socialist thinkers Proudhon has to be placed at the opposite extremity of Marx, and even, in this context, to Louis Blanc. His dominant passion was freedom. He was healthily scornful of 'Utopian systems', and called for the abolition of the State, or, at any rate, its reduction to one function—the organisation of credit and its distribution to the right people. That is, to the workers.

In reality Proudhon was probably still more Utopian than the Utopians he criticised. He wanted justice for all, based on the principle of reciprocity, which he saw as the only valid limitation to the freedom of the individual. Everybody could be free, on condition that he or she did not infringe anybody else's freedom. He called himself 'socialist', but he it was who first used the word 'anarchism' as it is now understood. He was against not only the centralised State that Louis Blanc advocated but also Fourier's model communities, in which he feared that equality would be forced on the inhabitants by a factitious majority. His best-known saying is famous: 'Property is theft.' As for elections and their outcome, elected assemblies, he was frankly hostile towards them, for there too he feared the tyranny of the majority and further infringements of liberty.

All this—this mixture or mish-mash—constitutes the various ingredients of 'socialism', starting with Saint-Simon's church, to Owen's, Fourier's and Cabet's communities, through Blanqui's violent revolution and proletarian dictatorship and finally Louis Blanc's 'democratic socialism' and Proudhon's anarchism. Each and all these conflicting ideas produced in turn movements, parties and factions, which we shall look at later.

NOTES

1 Emile Lehouck, *Vie de Charles Fourier* (Denoel/Gontier, 1978), p. 152.
2 Maurice Dommanget, *Auguste Blanqui des origines à la révolution de 1848* (Mouton, 1959), pp. 85–90.

2

Marx and Marxism

On Marx and Marxism, everything possible must have been said and said again, by the disciples, by the opponents and by objective students. I have no intention of offering a complete analysis of the Marxist phenomenon. I shall therefore limit myself to attempting to place Karl Marx's thought in the context of the socialist ideas of his time; from which it will be seen that, with some exceptions, he borrowed most of his ideas from those 'Utopians' whom he denounced with that ferocious intransigence that characterised him. But that is not the important point. When he borrowed ideas, Marx distorted them, or even turned them upside down. Where the idealists or 'Utopians' preached universal brotherhood, Marx preached hatred, envy and the class struggle. He alone had the key to history, he alone knew the unchanging 'laws' of society and of the economy. The 'others' were mere philosophers; he considered himself a man of science. In other words, he alone had the absolute truth. This conviction, along with his determination to 'change the world', made Marx the true point of origin of modern totalism.

MARX'S LIFE

In contrast to the early socialists—to Robert Owen, Fourier and the rest—Marx had a rather unpleasant character. With the one exception of his great friend Friedrich Engels, he quarrelled with everybody. He was undoubtedly a hard worker, but he was a scrounger and helped himself shamelessly to whatever came his way, not least to other people's money. Believing, presumably through pride, that the importance of his work relieved him of the duty to earn a living, he lived from loans, through subsidies from Engels, from a legacy of 6,000 francs which he had managed to extract from his mother before her death, and from authors' advances made available by his publishers, for books which he

16

did not have the slightest intention of writing. The father of a large family, he loved his wife and children (of whom several died young) in his own way, but in effect had sentenced them to live in the direst poverty. Moreover, he was responsible for the pregnancy of Lenchen Demuth, their faithful servant, who bore his child.

Marx's parents were Jews who had been converted to Protestantism. All his adult life, he was fiercely anti-Semitic. As a revolutionary, he was a thinker but not a very successful man of action. He was at his ease in small groups, which he dominated by the force of his personality. But he was not at home in crowds or assemblies and he made very few speeches. Organising riots, on the model of Blanqui, seemed to him a waste of time. His 'action' consisted mainly in an unending perusal of the bibliographical wealth of the British Museum. Having said that, he was one of the founders of the Communist League (the first true Communist Party), and, for a period, he dominated the First International. In general, however, action definitely took second place. Karl Marx was the ultimate intellectual.

Karl Marx was born at Trier in the Rhineland. He studied at Bonn University, then in Berlin (which at the time was dominated by the great philosopher of the State, Hegel), and finally at Jena, where he graduated as a Doctor of Philosophy. Aged 24, he became the Editor of the *Rheinische Zeitung* in Cologne, where he met Engels for the first time. But this assignment did not last long; some months later, the Prussian government imposed censorship and Marx resigned. In June 1843 he married Jenny von Westphalen, who was four years older than he, and whom he had known for seven years. Attractive and intelligent, Jenny came from a well-to-do family. Her father, in particular, was of a long line of soldiers and high officials. Nothing had prepared her for the life of misery which she would later know, especially in the London years.

In exile in Paris, Marx and Engels were active in communistic societies. They made no attempt to hide their revolutionary ideas and in February 1844, after an intervention from the Prussian government, Karl Marx was expelled by the French government. He took refuge in Belgium, still with Engels at his side. In fact, Engels was becoming more and more his indispensable companion. He had lived in Manchester, where his father had set up a textile workshop, which gave him a direct experience of 'capitalism'.

The two years they spent in Belgium were fruitful. Together they wrote *Die heilige Familie* (*The Holy Family*), a fierce attack upon the idealistic philosophy of the Hegelian theologian Bruno Bauer. This was followed by a vast volume, *Die deutsche Ideologie* (*The German Ideology*), which contained the first exposition in depth of their 'materialist' concept of history. Alas, nobody wanted to listen to them, still less to read them; and *Die deutsche Ideologie* remained unpublished during their lifetimes.

Already, Marx considered himself infallible. From now on, he would attack anybody who did not share his ideas, or who might be bold enough to contest his intellectual authority. He had begun with 'Bauer and his accomplices' (the sub-title of *The Holy Family*). Now he would turn on the other 'so-called philosophers', headed by Wilhelm Weitling. Weitling, of proletarian origin, was the intellectual leader of the German workers' movement. He had had the nerve to present the problems of society in *moral* terms. This was truly intolerable. Moreover, he asserted that the working class could reach communism directly, without going through the preliminary stage of a 'bourgeois' revolution. In a series of unbelievably violent articles, Karl Marx attempted to demolish the reputation of this false prophet.

His next target was none other than Proudhon, whose philosophy dominated socialist thought at that time. At first, Proudhon had established friendly relations with the young Marx. He had read a good deal and heard even more on the philosophy of Hegel, but he had no German. The presence of a 'Monsieur Marx' who happened to be in Paris, and who would surely be able to explain the thinking of the German philosopher was drawn to his attention. The year was 1844. Proudhon made the acquaintance of Marx, and the two men spent long evenings together, sometimes right into the morning hours. Marx was flattered. He praised Proudhon's 'vigorous style' and his 'bold new ideas, which will be epoch-making'.

Three years later, Karl Marx discovered that Proudhon was a rival. For anybody who wishes to be the uncontested prophet, the presence of other prophets is embarrassing. Short of being able to get rid of them physically, it was absolutely necessary to eliminate them intellectually. Marx made the attempt in 1847 in his book *La Misère de la philosophie* (translated into English as *The Poverty of Philosophy*), a biting and ironical reply to Proudhon's work, *Philosophie de la misère*. Proudhon wanted to unite the best aspects of contrary phenomena, such as competition and monopoly. He hoped to preserve the good aspects while eliminating the bad. Marx countered that no balance was possible between the antagonisms of this or that economic and social system. Social structures, he wrote, are merely the transitional historical forms determined by productive forces. Proudhon's reasoning, the reasoning of this self-taught '*parvenu* of science', was typical of this *petit bourgeois* who had failed to understand the fundamental laws of history.

Meanwhile, revolution was brewing at various points in continental Europe. In 1847, a secret society, the League of the Just, consisting mainly of German craftsmen in exile, gathered in London and decided to draft a political programme. An emissary was sent to Brussels to invite the collaboration of Marx and Engels. In June, Engels, travelling alone, had taken part in a Congress of the League in London, where it was decided to change its name. Henceforth, it was to be known as the Communist League. In November Marx decided to accompany Engels to the second Congress of the League, again in London. After some initial hesitation, they decided to undertake the drafting of the new Party's programme. It took them six weeks. In London, the revolutionaries were growing increasingly impatient, and even threatened to 'discipline' the two absent philosophers. Finally, the result was ready. Entitled *The Manifesto of the Communist Party*, the new programme was accepted enthusiastically. It was to become the most famous political pamphlet in all history.

For some time, Marx and Engels had been in the habit of referring to 'our theory', by which they believed they could give a complete and scientific explanation of the history of humanity. This theory is to be found, in its broad lines, in the *Communist Manifesto*.

The whole of history, they declared, was summed up in the history of the class struggle. The victory of the proletariat would bring the struggle to an end and usher in the era of the classless society. The *Manifesto* condemned all forms of socialism previously on offer, rejecting all Utopias, all communal experiments, as so many attempts to put a brake on, or to find a palliative in the class struggle. All of them, the *Manifesto* declared, were merely reactionary sects.

Ten measures were laid down, including a progressive income tax, the abolition of private inheritance and free education for all. So many steps on the road to communism and the *Manifesto* ended with these ringing words: 'The proletarians have nothing to lose but their chains. They have a world to win. Working men of all countries, unite!'

The Manifesto had hardly been published when revolution broke out in France, Italy, Germany and Austria. Expelled from Brussels, Marx reached Paris a few days after the events of 22 February 1848. He wondered whether the revolution, the *real* revolution, was on the point of breaking out. Neither he nor Engels could be sure. The main point was to prevent the elections which were being talked about. Marx decided to make common cause with Blanqui. There was talk of organising demonstrations in all the big towns. But in the end, their disappointment was total. The elections duly took place on 23 April, and no fewer than 9 million voters went to the polls. It was a day of triumph for 'bourgeois' democracy, but not for communism.

Marx now founded a 'Communist Party of Germany', with 300 members scattered in various countries. He infiltrated them back into Germany, well armed with revolutionary tracts. He himself decided to go back to Cologne, where he was welcomed as a democrat, the public being quite ignorant of the revolutionary trend of his recent thinking. He founded the *Neue Rheinische Zeitung* and, in collaboration with Engels, published hundreds of articles. He was always very careful not to mention such words as 'communism' and 'communist'. This was a first exercise in deception tactics.

Despite these precautions, Marx was brought to trial in Cologne for 'incitement to rebellion'. He conducted his own defence, and so well that he was acquitted; but he was expelled nevertheless. Despite 'our theory', despite his discovery of the unchanging laws of history, it was the counter-revolution that was triumphing everywhere. Even the 'bourgeois' and republican revolution was clearly failing, in France as in Germany. The King of Prussia, Frederic-William, reasserted his claims. In France, Napoleon III came to power.

Now it was the turn of Paris to want to see the last of Karl Marx, who thereupon took refuge in London, accompanied of course by the faithful Engels. This was the start of the most miserable period of his life. Living in two small rooms in Soho, the Marx family lived in dire poverty. For fourteen years (1850–64), Karl Marx, by now politically isolated, haunted the British Museum, harassed by his creditors. Engels, who had gone back to his father's workshop in Manchester, kept the Marx family alive, but only barely with his subsidies. In the long first phase, these were modest, but they became generous towards the end of this sad period when Engels was promoted to the management of his father's business.

Marx's political isolation came to an end in 1864 when the International Association of Workers (the First International) was set up in London. He was not involved in the preparatory work, but was invited to take part in the first Congress of the International. Pretty soon, he came to dominate it, by the force of his personality and ideas.

The Paris Commune brought Marx the international fame which he craved. To be sure, he had had nothing to do with the revolutionaries of 18 March 1871, who after the Prussian siege had been broken had set up their organisation in the capital. But this did not prevent him from claiming paternity over the Commune through the First International. Marx's propaganda, disseminated by the International, reached all corners of the civilised world, from Stockholm to Sydney. He emerged in the public mind as the hidden brain behind the revolution. Here, perhaps, was the first example of the technique of 'disinformation', which much later was to be perfected by the Soviet KGB. Overnight, Marx was world-famous. He was intoxicated by this new experience. For it was he who was being acclaimed, not Louis Blanc, the apostle of socialism, nor Bakunin, the Russian giant and revolutionary orator who saw the Paris Commune as the direct refutation of Marx's authoritarian theories.

Alas for him, once again his hopes were dashed. At the end of May, the Commune was smashed by the Army of the French Conservative leader Thiers. In a speech, Marx saluted the martyrs of the Commune: 'History offers no example to be compared to their greatness ...'

Back in London Marx found himself in the thick of a storm. His speech on the Commune had deeply shocked his British comrades within the International, especially George Odger, the trade union leader. Marx did not even attempt to mollify them. On the contrary, he hurled insults at them, calling them 'henchmen of the capitalists' and 'miserable wretches'. The trades unions pulled out of the International. Marx, on his side, was far more worried about what the Bakunists might have been up to. To be faced with hostility from the moderates of the Workers' Movement left him cold, but a challenge from the Left—that was a different story.

His rival had had the nerve to bring up the problem of freedom under socialism. Marx replied with a series of manoeuvres, pamphlets and libels. He charged Bakunin with plotting against him, with having committed crimes, and with having borrowed money from him. Bakunin, now past 60 and far from the events, listened and read quietly. In the end, deeply disappointed, he decided to quit the International, and indeed to retire.

From Marx's standpoint, this was not quite the victory for which he had hoped for he too was obliged to resign in the face of the general indignation of his erstwhile comrades. However, what did this matter! Since he had lost out, he was going to make sure there were no winners. Engels proposed that the headquarters of the International should be transferred from London to New York. A majority of the delegates accepted this curious proposal. Shortly, as Marx had calculated, the International simply disintegrated, for lack of members. Now everybody had lost. Disappointed though he was, Marx could offer himself the consolation of *Schadenfreude*: the happiness that comes from making others unhappy.

The net outcome of these events, however, was that they put an end to Karl Marx's political chances. Henceforth, he turned back to his family, and to the composition of the great work which he had planned for many years: *Das Kapital*. For a long time he had been in the habit of calling himself an 'economist', but it was not until 1859 that he published his first work on economics, *Zur Kritik der politischen Ökonomie* (*Towards a Critique of Political Economy*). It was a start, but it did not take him far enough. Now it was up to him to provide humanity with the definitive *proofs* of 'our theory' on the economic origins of all history.

The first volume of *Das Kapital* was published in Berlin in 1867. The second and third did not appear until after Marx's death, in 1885 and 1894, respectively. Marx had left them uncompleted, and it fell to the faithful Engels to finish off the master's work.

The last years of Karl Marx were made difficult by various health problems: he suffered from carbuncles, insomnia and nervous depression. His wife, too, fell ill, and died before him at the end of 1881. Their eldest daughter, Jenny, also died, in 1883. At last, on 14 March 1884, the creator of Marxism died in his turn, in London.

MARXIAN THOUGHT

Although a man of the nineteenth century Marx was undoubtedly the most influential political thinker of the twentieth, far ahead of his contemporaries and successors. This phenomenon is not to be explained by the intrinsic value of his thinking: the causes must be sought elsewhere.

One of the difficulties that confront the student of Marxism lies in the fact that never once, in the course of a life largely devoted to literary production, did Marx produce a straightforward statement of his philosophy. To grasp what he was trying to say one must find the bits scattered here, there and everywhere in the great mass of books, articles, pamphlets and letters (especially his plentiful correspondence with Engels, long censured by the Soviet publishers), and join them together to the best of one's ability. It is a thankless task and the reward is not exactly satisfactory. The ambiguities are plentiful. This has led to interminable scholastic quarrels, and to mutually exclusive interpretations. The disciples of Karl Marx are a long way from agreeing on just what the master's thinking really was.

Having said this, everybody is free to dip into the heap, as it were, and pull out his or her version of Marxism, whatever the Marxists may think of it. All, or nearly all, the principal elements of his philosophy are borrowings. Lenin himself said so in his short work, *The Teaching of Karl Marx* (1914). Thus Marx borrowed the dialectical method from Hegel, even though he turned it upside down. His system of political economy, based on the labour theory of value, came to him from the British economist Ricardo. As for his theory of the State and revolution, he took it, as one might expect, from the French revolutionary tradition. Even a fundamental point—the *Praxis*, to which we shall return—was borrowed from the dreams of those 'Utopians' whom he despised: Owen, Fourier, Cabet, Saint-Simon—not, in this instance, to distort them, but to expand them to infinity. These little communal experiments were entirely without interest to him. 'Philosophers,' he wrote, 'have only *interpreted* the world in various ways; the point however is to *change* it.'

To change the world, to transform it from top to bottom. It makes one wonder; or, depending on the person, is an incitement to action. Of all the thoughts of Karl Marx, this is without doubt the most important, the most explosive. It appeared, in its stark form, without elaboration, in his famous *Theses on Feuerbach*, which were written in 1845 but published posthumously. Despite the rather pretentious title, which calls up visions of vast, German-style volumes, they are merely short notes, 'hurriedly scribbled down for later elaboration, absolutely not intended for publication, but ... invaluable as a first document in which is deposited the brilliant germ of the new world outlook' (in Engels' words). The young Marx—he was only 27 at the time—had already proclaimed his revolutionary and millennarian ambition. He was going to transform the world. In this, of course, he was not entirely mistaken.

Marx and Engels even borrowed the slogans, whenever they found good ones. Thus 'the proletarians have nothing to lose but their chains' was borrowed from the French terrorist revolutionary, Marat. 'The workers have no homeland' was another Marat coinage. The two friends spoke of 'the exploitation of man by man', which they had taken from the Saint-Simonian, Bazard. 'Workers of all countries unite!' This clarion call, so often quoted, was sounded by the German ex-student Schapper, who had used it in London, in printed form, four months before the publication of the *Communist Manifesto*.[1] Even the famous formula of the 'dictatorship of the proletariat', which first occurs in Marx's works in his *Critique of the Gotha Programme* (1875), was not original. Long before Marx, Blanqui had had the same idea of a strictly temporary dictatorship, during which the revolution would carry out its essential work of destroying bourgeois structures. Plagiarism is a paying proposition in the hands of a partnership as redoubtable as that of Marx and Engels.

Let us, however, come back to the primary ideas, for whether or not they were borrowed, their influence is undeniable. The activism of the Marxists is summed up in the Marxian theory of the *Praxis*: the world is to be transformed by putting the theory into *practice*, that is by *acting*. Marx rejected totally the contemplative role of the philosopher. For Marxists theory and action are really one and the same. One of the lead-

ing British critics of Marxism, R.N. Carew Hunt, put it this way: theory
and action (or *Praxis*) 'stand in much the same relation to one another
as do faith and works in Christian theology'.[2]

In passing, it should be noted that the importance of ideology in the
eyes of communists stems essentially from Marx's view of the *Praxis*.
When Marxist writers produce ideological texts, their purpose is not, as
it is with most non-Marxist writers, merely to produce ideas for dis-
cussion, since ideology is itself a form of 'action'. In practice, although
this is not how Marxists would put it, ideology serves internally (that is,
within the Communist Party in opposition, or throughout the State if in
power) to enforce obedience, conformity and cohesion. In other words,
ideology has a *disciplinary* function. Externally (that is, beyond the
State boundaries of communist regimes), ideology fulfills parallel purposes: to subvert non-communist regimes; to achieve or maintain or restore the unity of the international communist movement; and to justify
Soviet dominion over other communist countries. In other words, externally, ideology has an *imperialist* function. The eleventh of the *Theses
on Feuerbach* (on *Praxis*) may thus be regarded as one of the theoretical
roots of communist totalism.[3]

In this whole process, poor Ludwig Feuerbach (1804–72), a modest
German idealist philosopher, is on his own. In his *Essence of Christianity* (1841), he declared himself against the 'enslavement' of men by
religion. But paradoxically, he did not deny the value of religion, which
earned him the epithet of 'pious atheist'. Man, he reasoned, alienates
himself by projecting upon a supreme being qualities that really belong
to him as a man. Having borrowed this idea, as usual, Marx distorted it,
as usual. Religion, he said, was but a product derived from the material
conditions of mankind. But Feuerbach, he thought, was wrong in thinking that material conditions determine what man is in his essence. (*Der
Mensch ist was er isst*, said Feuerbach in a famous aphorism: 'Man is
what he eats'). On the contrary, said Marx, these material conditions
determine the 'social being', that is, the life of the community.

Since we must make a choice, let us confine ourselves to considering
three other master-ideas of Karl Marx: the class struggle; the dialectic;
and the labour theory of value.

Of all Marxian ideas, it seems to me that the class struggle is the most
pernicious, for it trades upon envy and is a permanent incitement to
violence and conflict. In the first paragraphs of the *Communist
Manifesto* Marx and Engels reduce all history solely to the class
struggle. This is also the theme of the most eloquent passages in the first
volume of *Das Kapital*. If Marx had confined himself to noting the fact
that throughout history some people or groups of people (invariably in
the minority), control the means of power and rule over others

(invariably the great majority), he would have done no more than express in eloquent and impassioned language a truth which it was open to anyone to observe. But he did not content himself with merely observing: he wanted to change the world. *Praxis* enters the argument. In the context of the dialectic, the world is on course towards the inevitable revolution which will put the proletariat permanently in power. Since the other social classes will be abolished there will no longer be a class struggle, nor any further revolutions.

This brings us to the dialectic, as Marx understood it. Marx had conceived his 'dialectical materialism' by up-ending the master-idea of the great German philosopher of idealism, Hegel (1770–1831). He had written: 'In him [Hegel], the dialectic is walking on its head; all that is needed is to put it back on its feet to give it a perfectly reasonable physionomy.' In fact, it was not Hegel who first thought of the dialectical method with the aim of reaching the truth, but Plato. Each argument was to be opposed by another, which would then be opposed in its turn, so that errors would be progressively exposed. Hegel borrowed the dialectical concept and used it to explain the nature of the universe. He also borrowed from Plato the view that ideas are the only reality (and in this sense, is rightly classified as an exponent of 'idealist' philosophy). The highest, and only, reality was the Absolute, and all ideas were in process of change until the Absolute was reached, which itself was unchanging and permanent. Hegel's dialectical description of this process he called thesis, antithesis and synthesis. A proposition is affirmed: that is the thesis. Having been affirmed it is negated; that is, a contrary proposition is affirmed, which he called the antithesis. Then came the synthesis (which Marx called the 'negation of the negation'), incorporating what is true in both the thesis and the antithesis. The entire process is then repeated: the synthesis becomes the new thesis, to which an antithesis is found, both yielding in turn to a new synthesis. And so on, *ad infinitum*, until the Absolute, which contains no imperfections and is therefore permanent, is attained.

As the Hegelian dialect stood, it was a mystical and abstract concept. Marx sought to make it 'scientific' by substituting his materialism for Hegel's idealism. In his hands, thesis, antithesis and synthesis became stages of social development. Feudalism, for instance, was the thesis, changing gradually until cumulative changes produced contradictions that could only be solved by a 'negation'—that is, by qualitative or dialectical change. At that point, feudalism was replaced by capitalism, its antithesis, but capitalism in its turn was destined to develop increasing contradictions, until in the end it yielded to the synthesis of socialism. Once socialism has been reached, contradictions are eliminated: this is the Marxian version of Hegel's Absolute. (Marx used the terms 'socialism' and 'communism' without always differentiating between them. Thus he accepted the name of 'Communist League' to make the point that his party had nothing in common with the Socialist Party of Louis Blanc.[4])

Before leaving Hegel, it might be added that Hegel was, quite unconsciously, one of the forerunners of the totalist State. He saw the State as 'the Divine Idea as it exists on the earth' and prescribed its worship. Having said this, he added that the State, having reached its full maturity, would respect freedom of the individual. This conclusion was debatable, to say the least. One should not perhaps attribute too much to this conservative philosopher who lived a century or so before the totalists of the twentieth. But he has often been accused of giving the Nazi regime the seal of 'respectability', by providing war criminals with a philosophical justification of mass murders, for after all, all they were doing was obeying the orders of the State. By the same token, Hegel's thinking, as filtered through Marx, is discernible in the communist forms of totalism.

Using dialectical materialism, Marx boasted that he had invented a science of history, which he explained according to economic 'laws'. Everything in human life and in the evolution of societies was to be explained solely by the theory of economic forces, 'independently of the will' (of men). This was the principal theme in his *Critique of Political Economy* (1859). In the real world, great men have always played a primary role in historical events. Lenin was indeed one of the great proofs of this proposition. Without Lenin, it is hard to argue seriously that the Bolshevik Revolution would have been what it was, even if we admit that it could have taken place and succeeded without him. Moreover, Marx's simplistic view of history entirely brushes aside the important element of fortuitous circumstances, which sometimes play a determining part. Thus, if the German government had not decided, while the Great War was still in progress, to allow Lenin to return from exile in the famous sealed train that took him back to Russia, Marxism would possibly have been only one of the many variations of socialist thought in the nineteenth century.

Let us, however, get back to Marx's argument. At a certain stage of history, he claimed, a minority gains control over productive forces; this control enables it to exploit the labour of the majority. Convinced by his own interpretation of the dialectic, Marx envisaged the inevitable collapse of capitalism. He described the phases of the collapse, as he saw it, in his big work, *Das Kapital*. Whether they like it or not, capitalists will be obliged to exploit the working class, for the working class constitutes the source of their profits. Competition forces them to accumulate capital, which is concentrated in cartels, monopolies and trusts. The weaker capitalists are driven out and forced into the ranks of the proletarians. Machines and gadgets, to the extent that they reduce the demand for labour, create unemployment. Hence a reduction of profits, which obliges capitalists to intensify their exploitation of the working class, which is forced in turn to offer its labour at more and more disadvantageous rates. The misery of the masses deepens inevitably, until the point is reached where they are obliged to unite and overthrow the system.

The Marxian revolutionary model is beautiful, with the perfect symmetry of *a priori* thinking. Objectively, however, Marx's historical 'science' simply does not stand up to examination. The dialectical method 'works' only if arbitrary choices of category are made. Feudalism did not break down because of economic contradictions but because in most feudal societies the king—the strongest of the feudal warlords—eliminated or subjugated the barons or other feudal rivals of his power. 'Capitalism' did not spring whole into the world as the 'antithesis' or 'negation' of feudalism, but as the result of a complex process which included the violent disproof of the divine right of kings, the decadence of Rome, the emergence of the Puritan ethic, new inventions, the spirit of enquiry of the Renaissance, and so on. Nor is socialism necessarily the synthesis, still less the materialistic Absolute freed of contradictions. In real life, as distinct from the fantasy world of Marxism, the workers have not been driven progressively deeper into misery, but have become increasingly affluent consumers. Indeed, in the United States where trade unionism has been largely free of the Marxist element and even of non-Marxist socialism, the organised workers, concentrating upon the admittedly materialistic aim of getting the best possible deal for themselves by making capitalism work, have achieved unparalleled working class living standards. Marx, in fact, had got the whole thing wrong. He had failed to foresee the astonishing escalation of technology; had failed to allow for the rise and international spread of the trade union movement; and had been blind to the growth of liberal and democratic political parties in the industrialised countries, representing (as he would have seen it) the bourgeois values he so despised. In a more humble philosopher such failures of anticipation would be pardonable. But Karl Marx saw himself as a scientist with the key to History; and his followers credited, and still credit, him with infallibility as a prophet.

True, the 'capitalist' world underwent a period of mass unemployment and crisis in the depression of the 1930s, but partial answers, at least, were found to the 'contradictions of capitalism', which displayed an extraordinary capacity for self-correction that would have astonished Karl Marx. No one knows whether the present generalised crisis of the advanced countries, which is in part a consequence of the new industrial revolution of high technology, will resolve itself. But it is certain that socialism does not provide the remedy.

Marx had prophesied that the revolution would take place in the most advanced industrialised countries, such as England or Germany. The Russian Revolution would have puzzled him; that was the last place where he would have expected to see 'his' revolution. Moreover, the Tsarist despotism, quite clearly, had collapsed not because of the 'contradictions' of capitalism (although Russian industry, whatever Soviet propaganda may say about it, was already in full growth), but because of the disasters inflicted by the Germans on the Tsar's armed forces. In fact, the only communist revolutions that might be considered 'spontaneous'—for instance, in China and Vietnam—took place in countries where the 'capitalist' sector was relatively weak. In both those countries, the communists came to power not thanks to a proletarian revolution, but through a peasant insurrection motivated at least partially by that quality particularly despised by Marx—patriotism in the face of a foreign enemy. The same observation applies to Yugoslavia.

As for the other 'socialist' regimes, they were either imposed by the Red Army (as in Eastern Europe or North Korea), or were the results of teleguided *coups d'état* (as in Afghanistan, Ethiopia and South Yemen), or else they were the end result of insurgencies aided and controlled by the USSR (as in Angola, Mozambique, etc.). On Cuba, the Batista regime, threatened by Fidel Castro's guerrillas but in no great danger, collapsed in fortuitous circumstances in which the dictator's loss of will probably played the major part.

To my knowledge, history offers no single example of a regime in which capitalism has collapsed under the weight of its own 'contradictions', in accordance with the Marxian formula. What Marx and Engels were evidently incapable of imagining was the latent capacity of 'capitalist' countries to adapt themselves to changing circumstances by finding as best they can solutions to problems such as unemployment and inflation, by reducing the power of monopolies, by introducing social security programmes and by combining within their systems both private and public control over the means of production.

But the literal fulfilment of prophecies appears to be of little interest to the millennarian mind. The Marxist who calls himself such is obliged to swallow the contradictions of Marx's philosophy, the most pernicious of which is that between the inevitability of socialism and the identity of theory and *Praxis*: if socialism were inevitable, because determined by scientific laws independent of men's will, then there should be no need for the expectant to do anything but await its coming. But Marx was a revolutionary as well as a thinker. He is not content to wait for his 'laws' to prove themselves, but calls upon his followers to 'change the world'. Marx's followers are therefore in duty bound to do everything to make the prophecies come true, to hasten the breakdown of capitalism and the advent of the revolution.

Non-Marxists who have not studied Marxism often fall into the error of supposing that Marxists are basically reformers with the courage of their convictions—mere militants determined to remove the ills of the society in which they live, if necessary by force. But to think on these lines is fundamentally to misunderstand Marxism: the Marxist is basically *opposed* to reform, except on occasion for expedient reasons, because reforms, if successful, retard the processes of history and the advent of socialism. This does not prevent communists, however, from advocating reform if in opposition, or from initiating them if they share power within a coalition (as during the first phase of François Mitterrand's government), since it may be of advantage to a communist party to cultivate a false image of reformism or to appear to be working loyally with, say, socialist ministerial partners. But the end in view is invariable: the abolition of all non-Marxist societies and their replacement by 'socialism'.

For all its scientific pretensions, Marxism is as Utopian as the rival varieties of socialist philosophy which Marx roundly condemned (Saint-Simon, Fourier, Owen, etc.). We quote elsewhere the Yugoslav Milovan Djilas on this subject, but whereas we may contemplate the ideas of the 'Utopians' with irony and even with humour, this luxury would be out of place with the Marxian philosophy, precisely because of its commitment to *Praxis*. The Marxists want to transform their dream into reality by force, so we really do have to take them seriously.

The labour theory of value lies at the heart of Marx's economic thinking. The profit made by the capitalist is due entirely, according to Marx, to the labour of the proletariat. This profit—the surplus value—consists of the difference between the value of the articles produced and the necessarily minimum wage paid to the worker to enable him to survive with his family (the subsistence wage). This value represents the time that is 'socially necessary' to produce the articles which will then be offered for sale. Let us not waste any more time on this infantile theory which no bona fide economist takes seriously these days.

As for the Marxian theory of the State, that, too, is full of contradictions. Karl Marx claimed to be a lover of freedom. By this he meant that he was against despotism. Given that he attributed the oppressive character of the 'bourgeois' State (even in liberal England whose hospitality he enjoyed) to class antagonisms, the logic of his argument ought to lead to the conclusion that the State would cease to be necessary once socialism had abolished social classes. But this brings us to another contradiction—a sizeable one—for Marx advocated the necessity of a State after the revolution so that socialism could be built. But if all States are oppressive, could the socialist State possibly be an exception to the rule? Marx never fully faced up to this dilemma, still less did he resolve it.

The *Communist Manifesto* called for a massive programme of nationalisation—involving State-ownership of the land, banks, industries and transport; the direction of labour; and the centralised control of education. Clearly such a programme could not be implemented without a massive *expansion* of the organs of the State. Many years later, in the *Critique of the Gotha Programme* (1875), Karl Marx suggested that in time the period of State-communism that would follow the proletarian seizure of power from the bourgeoisie would yield to the Stateless communism of economic abundance: 'from each according to his ability—to each according to his needs'.

At the time of his death, Marx had been planning to write a book dealing with the development of the State from the family and private property. To this end he made extensive notes which Friedrich Engels later expanded into his book *The Origin of the Family: Private Property and the State* (1884), the most complete expression of Marx's ideas on the State. Engels dismisses the problem of the State under communism in a much-quoted, paralysingly opaque passage:

> Government over persons is replaced by the administration of things and the direction of the processes of production. The State is not 'abolished', *it withers away*. (Italics in original.)

Let us note in passing that the State in the Soviet Union, far from 'withering away', seems as strong as ever nearly seventy years after the revolution that was supposed to do away with it. It is surely fair to point out that, at this point, the Marxian dialectics simply broke down. For socialism (communism) is supposed to be the final synthesis that rounds off the dialectical progression from feudalism (thesis) and through capitalism (antithesis). The socialist 'synthesis' was supposed to bring the millennium, but for a phase (of indefinite duration), the State would be needed, both to build the economic base for abundance and to liquidate the bourgeois class, thus abolishing class antagonism (the foundation of the State in Marxian theory). Yet the difference between the phase of State-communism when the State would have greatly enhanced functions, and the classless communism of abundance, when the State would wither away, would clearly be enormous, implying no less a dialectical change than that from feudalism to capitalism, or from capitalism to socialism. Is the dialectic, then, to start all over again?

Marx does not say; neither does Engels. Thus in the end, the Marxian Utopia is no less vague than the Heaven or Paradise of the early Christians, whose legacy Marx had condemned as the opium of the people.

During his last years Marx began to wonder, and possibly to grow indignant, in the face of the evident lack of enthusiasm of English governments to conform with his theories. The masses should have been sinking deeper and deeper into misery; instead, their lot was actually being improved by successive reforms. He would have been hard put to explain the prosperity of proletarians in the capitalist countries during the twentieth century.

To sum up, *none* of the ideas of Marx was original, and *none* stands up to objective examination; moreover, *none* of his prophecies has come true. The balance is devastating. How, then, should one explain the persistence of Marxism and the resistance of Marxist groups in the face of the more and more striking demonstrations of the emptiness of their philosophy, or rather of their ideology? I believe the answer is to be found in the depths of human nature, for reasons in which baseness and idealism are in competition with each other. Here is a list of these reasons, as I see them:

(1) Marxism appeals to the basest sentiments of the human species: hatred, envy and covetousness.

(2) At the same time it also appeals to idealism by offering future happiness: the era of abundance to be known as 'communism'. And this future happiness will be the fruit of present-day efforts. First, socialism has to be 'built' (although this particular thesis really belongs to Lenin).

(3) Moreover, Marxism claims to offer a universal answer to the great questions of humanity and to religion.

(4) For any intelligent and ambitious man or woman, as distinct from the masses, Marxism—especially when accompanied by Leninism— offers the possible achievement of absolute and permanent power. True, the climb to power in a communist regime also carries risks (such as purges, punishment, the Gulag and even death); but ambitious people tend not to think a great deal on such matters: the main point is to reach total power.

(5) Last but not least, Marx as 'god' was fortunate enough to find his prophet in Lenin. The counter-religion of Marxism was transformed into a counter-church. Moreover, Marxism-Leninism became the State ideology, with all the immense resources of the Soviet apparatus at its disposal. Without these, Marxism would have remained relatively feeble.

In his grave, in Highgate Cemetery, the remains of the large bearded man welcomes pilgrims from the world over. Posthumously, he enjoys an enviable reputation, despite the setbacks of his life and the poverty of his philosophy.

NOTES

1. See Leopold Schwarzchild, *The Red Prussian* (London, 1948), p. 153; Sombart, *Der proletarische Sozialismus*, vol. I, p. 307 and p. 363; also Gustav Mayer, *Friedrich Engels* (American edn), p. 85.
2. In *The Theory and Practice of Comunism* (1950), Pelican edn (1963), p. 59.
3. Brian Crozier, *A Theory of Conflict* (1974), p. 53.
4. Leopold Schwarzchild, *op. cit.*, p. 129.

BOOK TWO

The Doers

3

The Totalists*

It was not by chance that Mussolini and Hitler were socialists before
declaring themselves to be 'Fascist', or 'Nazi' (which of course simply
means 'National-Socialist'). For just as with Leninist communism,
Fascism and National-Socialism have their roots in the doctrines of
Karl Marx who, as we have already said, found his 'own' ideas in those
of the 'Utopian' socialists, whom he affected to despise utterly.

Through an accident of history, Stalin's communist regime helped the
Western powers to destroy totally the Nazi regime of Hitlerian
Germany, with which, a few years earlier, he had signed a pact which
almost amounted to an alliance. Mussolini's Fascist regime, by then,
had been swept away by the Western armies. In the fervour of the war
and of the common victory, this very recent history was forgotten, and
the common ideological origins of the three men were clouded over.
With the aura of victory, the international Communist Movement,
dominated by the Soviet Union, had no difficulty in prolonging its campaign of anti-Nazi propaganda which had been interrupted by the
Hitler–Stalin pact of 23 August 1939 and was resumed only on 22 June
1941 when the German Army began its invasion of the USSR.
(Incidentally, Stalin was taken completely by surprise when Hitler
invaded the Soviet Union, despite the clear warnings of the Communist
spy Richard Sorge.) Things would have been different, to say the least, if
Hitler had won the war . . .

Since then, communist propaganda never tires of exposing and
denouncing the 'dangers' of an alleged revival of Nazism and Fascism,
slender though these are in the face of the enormous expansion of their
ideological cousin, communism. It is therefore not without interest to go
back to the common origins of the totalist phenomenon.

* See footnote on p. xiii.

If Marx and Engels were the first totalists among the 'dreamers', the first among the 'doers' was undoubtedly Lenin (1870–1924). If events are considered in their historical order, the Bolshevik Revolution took place in 1917, Mussolini's 'March on Rome' in 1922, and the advent of Hitler to power through the electoral process, in 1933.

THE ORIGINS OF LENINISM

In Tsarist Russia the proletarians were few, the peasants numerous. At first sight, the country hardly seemed ripe to achieve socialism, according to Marxist theory. In fact, the first socialist thinkers envisaged a society based on peasant communes. They called themselves 'populists', according to the doctrine of the writer Aleksandr Herzen (1812–70), who thought that Russia could well pass from feudalism to socialism while avoiding the stage of capitalism. In the decades of 1860 and 1870, the Russian populists lost their faith in peasant revolt and turned instead towards urban terrorism. Their first big success took place in 1881 with the assassination of Tsar Alexander II. Bakunin, the violent anarchist, helped Sergey Nechayev write his work *The Revolutionary Catechism*. The two agreed that the sole aim of the revolutionary was 'to annihilate all traditions, all orders and all classes of the State in Russia'.

Whereas in Russia Bakunin's disciples, who mostly belonged to the intellectual classes, pressed on with their terrorist attempts, the thinker Georgy Plekhanov (1856–1918), who was in exile in Geneva, became the first Russian Marxist of significance. Russia, he proclaimed, could in no way be an exception to the rules of History. The working class was already growing fast, and the revolution would be based upon it, in Russia as elsewhere. In 1883, he founded the first Russian Marxist organisation: *Osvobozhdeniye Truda*, or 'Group for the Liberation of Labour'.

In 1895, the friends of Vladimir Ilyich Ulyanov, who called himself Lenin, sent him to Geneva to make the acquaintance of Plekhanov. Full of enthusiasm, the young Lenin came back to the Russian capital to merge together the various little Marxist groups into a new organisation which he styled the 'Union for the Struggle for the Liberation of the Working Class'.

The young revolutionary, during his rather brilliant law studies, had read *Das Kapital* and, from 1889, began to call himself a Marxist. Under cover of practising his profession as a lawyer, he became an activist within the various revolutionary groups. His ally, after that fateful meeting with Plekhanov, was none other than the future leader of the Mensheviks, L. Martov. In December 1895, Lenin was arrested by the Tsarist police and exiled to Siberia; not long after, Martov joined him. During his five years in internal exile, Lenin married Nadezhda Krupskaya, who became his secretary and revolutionary comrade. The couple got together with Martov and Plekhanov when their period of exile ended. They went to Munich, where they founded a revolutionary newspaper, *Iskra* (*The Spark*), which helped to rally the various groups of Russian Marxists. Among Lenin's followers was a man with a name that was fated to play a special part in History: Trotsky (his real name was Leiba Bronstein, and who later called himself Lev Davidovich, 1879–1940).

Quite suddenly, Lenin broke with Plekhanov and with the whole Russian populist tradition. In 1902, in a short but striking work, *What is to be Done?*, he denounced the theory that capitalism was pushing the proletariat unavoidably in the direction of the socialist revolution. He called for the creation of a revolutionary party, which would have to be disciplined, centralised and destined by its very nature to become the 'vanguard of the proletariat'. This was the start of the era of weasel words, of political semantics. Nobody was ever going to ask the proletariat for its consent in recognising its 'vanguard' in Lenin's party. Similarly, the organisation of the party, which he described as 'democratic centralism' had no connection with democracy. Certainly, the decisions were going to be taken at the centre by a small directing group, the forerunner of the CPSU's Politburo, but the rank-and-file would have nothing to do with such decisions, and would not even be consulted. This was the true beginning of the totalist State.

At its second Congress in 1903, the *Iskra* group split, and Lenin found himself in the minority. Luckily for him, one of the groups, known as the Bund and consisting of social-democratic Jews, decided to walk out of the Congress. Lenin, always the supreme man of action and decision, took advantage of this situation immediately by declaring that his own group was henceforth the majority group. To make the point absolutely clear, he decided that his group would henceforth be known as the 'Bolsheviks' (meaning 'majority' in Russian). The others, the minority group in absentia, would be named 'Mensheviks' (or 'minority' in Russian). It was thus that the ground rules of the future Soviet Union were laid, according to which the opposite of the truth becomes the official truth. As for Lenin's party, at least during this gestation period, its official name was the Russian Social-Democratic Workers' Party.

There is no point in recalling the interminable factional quarrels within the Social-Democratic Party. In Prague in 1912, Lenin announced that henceforth the Bolsheviks would alone constitute the Party. As for the Mensheviks, they were stigmatised as 'schismatics'. Starting from Karl Marx, Lenin passed naturally to intellectual totalism, which soon became political totalism. He alone, as with Marx in his day, held the absolute truth. It was as the leader of the Bolsheviks that Lenin would seize power in November 1917 from the feeble hands of Kerensky. The dream was over; the nightmare of socialist reality was beginning. This nightmare is still with us. To the extent that the aberrations of the Soviet State are part of totalist communism, I shall only mention them in passing. In a later chapter, we shall take a closer look at the economic and social achievements and realities of *socialism* in the USSR.

MUSSOLINI THE MARXIST

The son of a blacksmith, Benito Mussolini (1883–1945) was a kind of revolutionary layabout. Violent and rowdy, he was expelled from school three times: first from his primary school at Predappio in central Italy, then from the school of the Salesian Fathers at Faenza, where he was a boarder, and finally from the Giosuè Carducci at Forlimpopoli for attacking another pupil with a penknife. Despite this latest incident, he passed his exams without any trouble.

Strangely in the circumstances, Mussolini then became a school-master in his turn, but he soon recognised that he was hardly made for the job. Aged 19, the young Benito, a pallid chap with huge liquid black eyes, went to live in Switzerland. A significant detail was that his pockets were empty, except for a nickel medallion of Karl Marx. For some months, he lived a curious alternating life, sometimes as a tramp and sometimes as a daily labourer, sleeping in the open and raping any girls who were rash enough to turn down his advances.[1] At the same time, he was devouring, though not always assimilating, the works of Marx, Hegel, Kropotkin, Sorel and Nietsche.

Back in Italy in 1904, he soon attracted attention by making speeches in the street, in which he called on the workers to strike. He had another spell as a schoolmaster, this time in a village in the Venetian Alps, but led a rather debauched life and is said to have caught syphilis. As was true of Blanqui, Mussolini spent a good deal of his time in gaol.

He fell in love, in his fashion, with the daughter of his father's mistress, named Rachele Guidi and aged 16. He managed to seduce her, and married her in 1909. After a fifth spell in prison, he became a militant socialist and turned to journalism. Indeed. he founded his own newspaper, the title of which is surely significant: *La Lotta di Classe* (*The Class Struggle*). His Marxist convictions are not in doubt; in any case, he made no attempt to hide them. He sang the praises of the 'father and master' of the proletarian movement. He defended the doctrine of the pauperisation of the working class—the most contested of the Marxist theses. The class struggle, the expropriation of the bourgeoisie, the collectivisation of the means of production and exchange: such were the recurring themes of *La Lotta di Classe*, whose four pages daily were all written by Mussolini himself, and of the official socialist newspaper *Avanti!*, of which he became the Editor, and whose circulation rapidly soared.

As was true of most of the socialists of that time, Mussolini opposed Italy's entry in the First World War. When, despite everything, Italy did enter the war in 1915, he went so far as to call on Italian soldiers to desert. In fact, his initial attitude was much the same as that of Lenin, who was insisting that Tsarist forces should lay down their arms. True, at a later date, Mussolini changed his mind and started to preach war to the end, but the contrast between his new and bellicose attitude and Lenin's revolutionary pacifism was more apparent than real. The Russian saw in the military defeat of Tsarism the revolutionary opportunity he had waited for; the Germans had seen in Lenin's pacifist attitude the possibility of a change that would rid them of the enemy to the East. Had Lenin's attitude been bellicose, the Germans would never have allowed him to return to Russia in the famous armoured train which they had put at his disposal. Mussolini, on his side, had taken note of the fact that the war had facilitated the Bolshevik Revolution. From this fact, he drew a lesson for Italy, and of course for himself in the framework of his revolutionary ambitions.

Whatever his motives, Mussolini's change of attitude deeply shocked his socialist comrades, who expelled him from the Party. Using funds, the origin of which is still obscure, he founded a new paper, *Il Popolo d'Italia*, and proclaimed his new nationalist doctrine. This was the birth of Fascism.

In a remarkable work, *The Three Faces of Fascism*[2] the German historian Ernst Nolte drew a parallel between Mussolini and Lenin. Like Lenin, Mussolini intended to create socialism by means of the revolutionary path, by destroying the bourgeoisie and parliament. Like Lenin, he advocated an alliance between the workers and the peasants. True, Mussolini had criticised the Brest–Litovsk Peace, in which he saw a kind of betrayal of socialism, but six months later he was praising the leader of the Bolshevik Revolution. In 1921, however, he was critical of Lenin's New Economic Policy, which he feared might mean the abandonment of socialism. On the other hand, Mussolini envied the speed with which Lenin and his companions had mobilised all means of propaganda to serve the revolution. He would use this as his model after the violent and fraudulent elections of 1924 which laid the foundations of Fascist dictatorship. In Italy as in Russia, totalism started with socialism.

In the eyes of socialist historians and thinkers, Mussolini ceased to be a socialist from the time of his expulsion from the Party, and especially from a meeting on 23 March 1919 in Milan, where a handful of 'interventionist' Leftists (that is, those who favoured Italy's entry into the First World War) set up the Fascist Party. It is true that by abandoning proletarian internationalism, Mussolini had opted for unfettered nationalism. He had had the socialist deputy Matteotti murdered, and had started repressing the Socialist and Communist Parties.

Nevertheless, there are many points in common between the Soviet and Fascist regimes. They resemble each other far more than either resembles any parliamentary democracy. Moreover, it would be wrong to conclude that by creating his own party and establishing his dictatorship, Mussolini had abandoned the socialist ideas that had inspired his youth.

Of course, he had not gone so far as to destroy private enterprise, as Lenin and especially Stalin did. Instead of destroying the big companies he controlled them, together with the trades unions, through his 'corporations'. As far as the workers were concerned, he prohibited strikes from 1926. (In the USSR, strikes have never been formally prohibited, but in practice they are always repressed on the pretext that in the proletarian State where all enterprises are supposed to belong to the working class, striking is a nonsense; a sophistry which does not hide the grim reality beneath.)

The world depression, starting in 1929, gave Mussolini the pretext he was hoping for, to centralise and socialise his country's economy. In 1933, he created the *Istituto per la Ricuperazione Industriale* (IRI) with the aim of extending State participation in banking, insurance and industry. Officially this was not called 'socialism'. But in reality, the economy of Fascist Italy was a directed economy, and therefore a socialist one.

HITLER THE MARXIST

Even in the 1920s, Hitler (1889–1945) recognised a certain affinity between Nazis and Communists. Indeed, he had written:

> In the ranks of us National Socialists, the disenchanted of Right and Left must come together. All of them must learn that there is one place in Germany where faith in the future is far from lost. . . . in our movement the two extremes come together: the Communists from the Left, and the officers and students from the Right. These two have always been the most active elements, and it was the greatest crime that they used to oppose each other in street fights. The Communists were the idealists of Socialism.[3]

In the collection of his sayings entitled *Table Talk*, Hitler exclaimed:

I do not blame little men for becoming Communists; but I do blame the intellectual who has done nothing except exploit the poverty of others for other aims . . . I find the Communists a thousand times more sympathetic than Starhemberg [the leader of the Austrian Right], for example.

Hitler admired Stalin as 'one of the most extraordinary personages of world history'. 'An animal, but an animal of great stature,' he remarked. 'Stalin deserves our unconditional respect.'

Hitler envisaged the future revolution in terms which could have been accepted without demur by the communists:

A revolution has three main objectives. First of all, it is a matter of breaking down the partitions between classes, so as to enable every man to rise. Secondly, it is a matter of creating a standard of living such that the poorest would be assured of a decent existence. Finally, it is a matter of acting in such a way that the benefits of civilisation become common property . . . The people who call themselves democrats blame us for our social policy as if it were a kind of disloyalty; according to them, it imperils the privileges of the owning classes. They regard it as an attack on liberty; for liberty, in their view, is the right of those who have power to continue to exercise it . . . In virtue of what law, divine or otherwise, should the rich alone have the right to govern? The world is passing at this moment through one of the most important revolutions in human history.[4]

The admiration which Hitler felt for Stalin and for his iron regime went as far as plain emulation. Having succeeded Lenin in 1924, and made himself the uncontested master of the USSR after the expulsion of Trotsky in 1929, Stalin had a much longer experience of the techniques of extermination than Hitler. Shortly after the invasion of Russia by the German armies Stalin took advantage of it to deport or massacre whole populations, especially from the Caucasus and the Ukraine. In this respect Hitler was a good pupil, and imitated Stalin's example with the genocide of the Jews.

In both cases, moreover, the intellectual genesis is identical. With very few exceptions, present-day socialists, even those who call themselves Marxists, ignore or keep silent about the anti-Semitism of Marx and Engels. Yet appropriate quotations are not lacking. Marx and Engels advocated the liquidation not only of certain social classes but of whole nations, which they considered essential to any advanced doctrine of scientific socialism.[5] In January and February 1849, for example, Friedrich Engels published an article in Karl Marx's paper, *Neue Rheinische Zeitung*, in which he proposed the extermination of entire races in Europe. Some months after Lenin's death, Stalin published his book *The Foundations of Leninism* (1924), in which may be found eulogistic quotations from the article by Engels. The Soviet State, Stalin argued, would be obliged to destroy entire peoples because they stood in the way of the revolution. He explained the attitude of Marx and Engels by placing it in its historical context. At the time, the Poles were considered a revolutionary people, whereas the Czechs and the southern Slavs were 'reactionary'. It was therefore necessary to liquidate the latter. According to Stalin, the peoples destined to be liquidated in the name of the revolution included, among others, the Highland clans in Scotland, the Bretons, the Basques and the Yugoslavs.

Had Hitler read the Engels article and Stalin's book? It is impossible to answer with certainty, but what is certain is that the two texts were both available to him. The Staatsbibliothek in Munich had acquired the text of the Engels article in 1901, and it had been reproduced in a book by Franz Mehring published in 1913, the very year when Hitler, always an avid reader, had settled in Munich. Likewise, Stalin's book had been translated into German in the year of its original publication under the title *Lenin und der Leninismus*, and was published in Vienna while Hitler was in gaol for his part in the failed *Putsch* of the previous year. It was during this period of forced inactivity that Hitler wrote the first volume of *Mein Kampf* while he was devouring historical and political texts that were placed at his disposal by his tolerant warders.

Was Hitler a Marxist? In the full sense of the word, he was certainly a good deal less so than Mussolini. He denounced Bolshevism as a Jewish conspiracy and claimed to be leading a crusade against it. Yet according to several well-authenticated quotations, he also saw no incompatibility, or very little, between Bolshevism and Nazism. But then, intellectual consistency was never among his characteristics. In 1934, he had declared:

> It is not Germany that will turn Bolshevist but Bolshevism that will become a sort of National Socialism ... Besides, there is more that binds us to Bolshevism than separates us from it ... I have always ... given orders that former Communists are to be admitted to the Party at once. The *petit bourgeois* Social Democrat and the trade union boss will never make a National Socialist, but the Communist always will.[6]

In fact, more than half the 50,000 Brownshirts recruited in the previous year were former communists.[7] Goebbels, the Nazi propaganda chief, could just as easily have become a communist as a Nazi, and had expressed boundless admiration for Lenin. In reality, communism and National Socialism were not incompatible but *in rivalry* with each other; their 'recruiting catchment' was essentially the same.

Public opinion in the Western countries was deeply shocked by the 'incredible' news of the Hitler–Stalin (or Ribbentrop–Molotov) Pact, signed in Moscow on 23 August 1939, but in Germany as in the Soviet Union, the propaganda services of the two totalist States had no difficulty in switching from mutual insults to mutual praise. Stalin's recompense was the occupation of the Baltic States and of eastern Poland. Very swiftly, a close and indeed logical collaboration was formed between the secret services of the two regimes, the Gestapo and the NKVD, the predecessor of the KGB.[8]

There is an unfortunate tendency in Western countries to forget what happened thereafter. On 11 February 1940 Molotov and Ribbentrop signed a pact of another kind, a commercial agreement, under which the USSR exported to Germany one million tons of grain, 900,000 tons of oil, 100,000 tons of cotton, 500,000 tons of phosphates, 100,000 tons of chrome and 500,000 tons of pig iron. On their side the Germans provided the Soviets with a large quantity of arms. Stalin has never been accused of naïveté, but it is certain that he considered Hitler as his ally, and that he was taken by surprise by the invasion of 22 June 1941.

The crimes of Nazism are universally known and I shall not recall them in detail here. I confine myself to recalling a less well-known aspect of the Nazi regime—the fact that the economy of Hitler's system was incontestably a *socialist* economy. It was also a *war* economy, just as the Soviet economy has always been at once a socialist and a military economy.

In the first phase, Hitler (who had no interest in economic questions but who did intend to mobilise the people) smashed unemployment with dazzling speed, by means of an intensive programme of public works and generous tax concessions to companies ready to increase their investments in machine tools and especially in armaments. In 1932 Germany had nearly six million unemployed. Within four years the figure dropped to less than a million.

The very clever Dr Schacht, 'Plenipotentiary-General for the War Economy' from May 1935, was the wizard, the master-manipulator of credit. The German mark had 237 different exchange rates according to the country and the circumstances. But Schacht did not last very long and resigned in 1937. Meanwhile the Number 2 of the Third Reich, Hermann Goering, had become the economic dictator and had launched a Four-Year Plan. Small companies (with a capital value not exceeding $40,000) were abolished and merged into the great cartels. The multiplicity of forms to be filled was the despair of businessmen who, however, enjoyed increasing profits as official orders were stepped up. The State managed everything, and the heads of private enterprise soon discovered that all power of decision had been taken away from them. One of the best known, Fritz Thyssen, whose personal fortune had helped to swell the coffers of Nazism, chose to flee when war broke out. 'The Nazi regime has ruined German industry,' he declared. 'What a fool [*Dumkopf*] I was!' he would often exclaim in future years.[9]

Just as in Russia and in Italy, the workers had lost their freedom. Strikes were forbidden, of course, and the worker, as with the serf in Tsarist Russia, was tied to his master, the boss, in a sort of mediaeval slavery. He earned less than before the advent of Hitler, to the extent that despite the fall in unemployment, the workers' share of the gross national product had declined from 56.9 per cent in 1932 to 53.5 per cent in 1938, the boom year. As in the USSR, the worker was not allowed to change his job or his residence. The agricultural workers, on their side, were denied the right to leave their farms and seek their fortunes in the towns. Incidentally, the peasants were a good deal more successful than factory workers in escaping from these repressive laws. In the view of the great American historian of the Nazi regime, William L. Shirer, between 1933 and 1939 more than a million agricultural workers left the farms to find jobs in the towns. The urban workers were under closer surveillance and bore the brunt of the repressive character of German socialism.[10]

It would be an error to draw from these examples the conclusion that socialism leads inevitably to dictatorship and repression. But the conclusion is inescapable that all regimes based on Marxism or upon the integral application of socialist principles have in fact become repressive dictatorships. Where social-democratic parties have come to power, and where the respect for the principles of democracy (in particular that of the alternation of parties in power) has been given priority above the creation of socialism, the infringement of freedom is much less, to the extent that socialism is seen as a temporary phenomenon. One of my 'Universal Rules' therefore emerges: the more socialism, the less freedom.

NOTES

1 Christopher Hibbert, entry on Mussolini in *Encyclopaedia Britannica*, (Chicago, 1975), Macropaedia, Vol. 12, p. 750.

2 *Der Faschismus in seiner Epoche* (Munich, 1963), (New American Library, USA, 1969).

3 Quoted by Tibor Szamuely, a Soviet defector, in *We Will Bury You* (London, 1970).

4 Adolf Hitler, *Table Talk, 1941–1944*, edited by Hugh Trevor-Roper, translated by Norman Cameron and Robert Stevens (London, Weidenfeld & Nicolson, 1953).

5 See in particular, Paul Johnson, 'Marxism vs the Jews' in the New York review, *Commentary* (April 1984); George Watson, 'Race and the Socialists' in the London review, *Encounter* (November 1976) and 'Was

Hitler a Marxist?' in the same publication (December 1984). A fuller analysis appears in Leslie R. Page's *The Marxian Legacy: Race, Nationalities, Colonialism and War* (The Freedom Association, London, 1983).

6 Hermann Rauschning, *Hitler Speaks* (T. Butterworth, London, 1939), p. 134.

7 Eliot B. Wheaton, *Prelude to Calamity: The Nazi Revolution 1933–35* (London, 1969), p. 436. See also Nikolai Tolstoy, *Stalin's Secret War* (Cape, London, 1981), pp. 86–7.

8 Tolstoy, *op. cit.*, pp. 103, 229, 292. See also Alfred Seidl (ed.), *Die Beziehungen zwischen Deutschland und der Sowjetunion 1939–1941*, (Tübingen, 1949).

9 William L. Shirer, *The Rise and Fall of the Third Reich* (Secker & Warburg, London, 1959–63), p. 261.

10 William L. Shirer, *op. cit.*, p. 265.

4

Democrats and Franquists

During the last decade of the nineteenth century and the first few of the twentieth, the history of socialism may be summed up in terms of disputes over doctrine and tactics. The notion of 'socialism' as an idea or a dream being taken for granted, the important thing is to choose the right road, first to put socialists into power and secondly to create 'socialism' (whichever definition of it is accepted, according to the country and the circumstances, the parties and their leaders).

I shall not linger too long over these disputes.[1] They concern essentially a fundamental point: is it possible to inaugurate socialism without revolution? On this point, even Karl Marx's thinking had undergone changes. The great apostle of violent revolution had asked himself whether violence was going to be necessary after the Reform Bill had passed through the English Parliament in 1867, and had reached the stage of suggesting that a peaceful evolution towards socialism might be possible, at least in the cases of England and the United States.

In Germany Ferdinand Lassalle (1825–64), the architect of the trade union movement, wanted to call upon the government to provide the workers with enough capital to set up co-operatives, and thus emancipate them from capitalist domination. For Marx the idea of any kind of appeal to the bourgeois State was monstrous, and he denounced Lassalle in venomous terms ('that Jewish negro Lassalle,' he wrote in a letter to Engels on 30 July 1862). Karl Kautsky (1854–1938), theoretician of social democracy, was a determinist: since socialism was inevitable, all that was needed was to wait for it. The revisionist Eduard Bernstein (1850–1932) called on socialists for an explicit renunciation of all 'revolutionary baggage'. In Germany, he said, it was possible to reach socialism without violence.

In France the Marxist tendency clashed with certain very French traditions. The Workers' Party of Jules Guesde (1845–1922) represented

46

Marxist orthodoxy, in contrast to the theses of Blanqui and Proudhon (which in any case were contradictory), both of them proud of having taken part in the Paris Commune. Between the revolutionists and the evolutionists, there was no common ground. Guesde did not disdain social reforms, but considered them as mere platforms for agitation. This attitude clashed with the evolutionism of the great orator Jean Jaurès (1859–1914), founder of the Unified Socialist Party.

The First International, that of Marx and Engels, having disintegrated, the second wave dreamers created a Second International in 1889. There, at last, the German socialists who predominated, could indulge to their hearts' content in their scholastic quarrels and in particular could reproach Jean Jaurès for advocating a socialist participation in a 'bourgeois government'. This luxury, in any case, did not cost very much, since in Germany at least there was no question of any such participation.

In their speeches and debates the socialists of that period all paid homage to the internationalism of the working class—until the Great War broke out in 1914. Jaurès, who was a pacifist, was assassinated on the eve of the war. In Germany as in France the 'working class' discovered its own fatherland, which did not transcend national frontiers. In general all socialist parties, on both sides of the Rhine, became patriots and supported the war. Despite the moving eloquence of pacifist resolutions the International did not stand up to the sadly visible collapse of working class solidarity.

After the war everything had to start again from scratch. In any case, a new element, of truly transcendental importance, upset all preconceptions: the Bolshevik Revolution, which was seen as the apparent triumph of the violent road towards socialism. The Third International (or Comintern), created by Lenin in 1919 set itself a well-defined world mission. It was intended to be the instrument destined to spread communism, on the Soviet model, to all countries of the world without exception.

Everywhere, in Europe, in Asia, in Africa, in Latin America, the Comintern set up Communist Parties. In France it was well served by the splits within the Socialist Party. At the Congress of Tours, towards the end of 1920, four tendencies manifested themselves in competition with each other: the extreme Left, the Left, the Centre Right and the Right. The Extreme Leftists, headed by Maxime Leroy, favoured the immediate entry without reservations into the Third International. The Leftists, among whom were the names of future leaders of the Communist Party such as Marcel Cachin and Paul Vaillant-Couturier, also advocated membership, but with certain adjustments. The Centre Right, led by Robert-Jean Longuet and Paul Faure, refused to join; the

Right, within which the dominant personality was that of Léon Blum, also declined to join, without any thought of compromise. The results of the Congress of Tours are now part of history. The Left and the extreme Left between them were in the majority. Those who favoured membership of the Third International won the day and the Party changed its name. Henceforth, it was to be the *Communist* Party. The new majority inherited the daily which Jaurès had edited, *L'Humanité*, which from that point on was the Communist organ. As for the minority of the Right and Centre Right, it managed, more or less, to rebuild the Socialist Party, the organ of which would be *Le Populaire de Paris*. In France as elsewhere, the Communists denounced their erstwhile brothers in vehement terms: as social traitors, traitors to the working class, and so forth.

In Britain, the socialist Left almost entirely escaped this kind of traumatic experience. The Communist Party, created by the Comintern in 1920, remained fairly feeble, as indeed was the Marxist tradition. In 1900 various more or less socialist groups, consisting of small socialist parties (such as Keir Hardie's Independent Labour Party), of trades unions and of co-operatives, gathered in London and constituted the Labour Representation Committee. The Committee put up candidates for the parliamentary elections and even had some successes. In 1906 after the landslide of David Lloyd-George's Liberal Party, the Committee transformed itself into a full-blown party. Thus was the Labour Party born.

From the start there was a dose of Marxism in the Labour Party, but initially it was rather weak. There was also a measure of Owenism, and the ideas of the painter William Morris, who favoured a kind of 'craftsman's socialism'. The British Labour Movement was a response to a certain social unease in respect of the least-favoured class; poverty shamed highminded middle-class people and the churches in general, especially the Methodists. The idea was to press for wage increases and improvements in working conditions through the trades unions. Poverty would be abolished not only through social reforms but especially through a programme of redistribution of wealth.

The intellectual inspiration for the Labour Movement sprang above all from the Fabian Society, founded in London in 1883 by a small group of young intellectuals. Why 'Fabian'? Because the Roman consul, Maximus Verrucosus, known as Fabius Cunctator—the Delayer), knew all about caution and waiting tactics. His prudence had brought to a halt the advances of the redoubtable Hannibal. The British Fabians, likewise, felt they knew all about the virtues of patience. Their slogan, frequently quoted, amounted to a whole philosophy: 'The inevitability of gradualism'. All you had to do was to wait until socialist ideas spread like an oil stain. Thus socialism would be built little by little, without violence, in the gentleness of time. Those who feared socialism—and they were numerous—retorted that gradualism would in no way reduce the disadvantages of socialism, once it had been attained.

The most famous of the Fabians were the writers George Bernard Shaw (1856–1950) and H. G. Wells (1866–1946). Shaw, who was only 28 when he joined the Society and was still unknown, was not in the true sense a political figure, but he was an excellent publicist and propagandist. Once he became famous he was read and listened to because his plays dominated the London theatre. As for Wells, the prophet of a Utopia of technocrats and scientists and the forerunner of space exploration and 'Star Wars', he did not lack originality in his thinking, and during several decades enjoyed an enormous audience. It is true, however, that television did not yet exist. The dominant influences within Fabianism, however, were those of Sidney and Beatrice Webb (respectively, 1859–1947 and 1858–1943), those indefatigable encyclo-paedists of the trades unions and municipal councils.

It was a curious fact that these apostles of gradualism were fascinated by the Soviet experiment. Shaw and Wells had both visited the Soviet Union, had seen what Stalin wanted them to see, and had come back full of enthusiasm. They had 'seen the future' and convinced themselves that it worked. As for the Webbs, they spent several months in the USSR and wrote an enormous tome to explain that Stalin and his comrades had found the solutions for all the problems of society. In its first edition, this massive work—which today is a real museum piece—was entitled *Soviet Communism: a New Civilisation*? After a second trip they decided to delete the question-mark. They had seen nothing of the Gulag, nor of the famine wholly created by the policies of the dictator in the course of which *well over ten million* peasants had found their deaths.[2] Even the French writer, André Gide, had shown himself more aware of realities when he wrote his book, *Return From the USSR*.

Once again, let us leave the dreamers and look at the doers. At the end of 1923 the British government led by the Conservative Stanley Baldwin fell, and general elections brought the Labour Party to power for the first time. The Scotsman, Ramsay MacDonald (1866–1937), the illegitimate son of a servant girl who went on to be a teacher, was appointed Prime Minister. In Marxist terms the petty bourgeoisie had come to power. So had the working class incidentally, for some of his ministers, in particular the Home Secretary, Arthur Henderson, were sons of manual workers. The government took office on 22 January. One of its first acts was to recognise the Soviet regime *de jure* ten days later. A commercial agreement followed.

To be frank, this first 'achievement' on the part of socialists was a failure, and the experiment did not last long. The government discredited itself by arresting J. R. Campbell, the editor of a communist paper, *Workers' Weekly*, who was charged with sedition. He was a bad choice for victim, for he was a crippled World War One veteran and had been awarded the Military Medal for gallantry. He was soon freed following a wave of protests from the extreme Left. Having lost a vote of confidence in the House of Commons MacDonald resigned. Leaving aside the establishment of diplomatic relations with the Soviet regime, his balance sheet was on the thin side: a law, much praised, obliging the municipal authorities to put modest housing at reasonable rents at the disposal of the workers.

During the electoral campaign the so-called 'Zinoviev letter' caused a sensation. The letter apparently came from the Comintern and was signed by one of Stalin's assistants, Zinoviev. It deliberately incited the workers to revolt. Almost certainly the Zinoviev letter was a forgery. Whether it was or not MacDonald panicked and his party was crushed in the elections in October.

Labour would wait six years for a second chance, during which the most important event in domestic policy was the General Strike of 1926, the last spasm of the partisans of revolutionary violence. Back in power in June 1929 MacDonald and his friends were soon overwhelmed by the Wall Street crash and the world depression which swiftly followed. The Labourites had had themselves elected on an ambitious programme of social reforms, but in the face of a rapid rise in unemployment and a disastrous flight of capital MacDonald lost his nerve and failed to implement it. The business world insisted on a balanced budget and a cut in unemployment benefits. MacDonald dithered and the trades unions came out against 'their' government. Taken aback, MacDonald changed direction. He quit the Labour Party and became Prime Minister of a coalition government of Tories and Liberals. Some of his colleagues crossed the floor with him. Howls of anguish followed from the socialist movement: MacDonald was duly dubbed a traitor to the working class. That was the end of the socialist experiment between the two World Wars.

In Germany the Social Democrats, although in a minority, came to power in 1928 after the May elections, and their leader Hermann Müller (1876–1931) was appointed Chancellor. He too, like MacDonald, was overwhelmed by the Wall Street crash and the economic depression. In Sweden alone, during this difficult period, a socialist government could claim that it had brought unemployment under control with a programme of public works and centralised planning.

In 1935, clearly worried by the inexorable rise of Hitler and to a lesser extent by Mussolini's imperial ambitions, Stalin gave new marching orders to the Communist International. At the Seventh Congress of the Comintern in Moscow on 23 July, under the chairmanship of the famous Bulgarian leader Georgi Dimitrov—hero of the Reichstag fire trial—the ideas and slogan of the 'Popular Front' were launched. Dimitrov defined it as an electoral alliance between the 'parties of the working class' and the 'anti-Fascist bourgeois elements'. Henceforth, the European Communist Parties would never tire of proposing to the Socialist or Social-Democratic Parties (or in France, for example, to the Radicals), the creation of 'Popular Fronts' against Fascism.

In 1933 the French Communists had denounced the Socialists in vehement terms for supporting radical governments; now, they offered reconciliation. At first the Socialists hesitated. But the Stavisky financial scandal and the popular riots of February 1934 had a chastening effect.

On 14 July 1935 the alliance of the Left was consummated with gigantic street processions. Fairly tough negotiations between the Communist, Socialist and Radical parties followed. On 11 January 1936 the Left published a common programme for a new 'Popular Rally'. It caused a sensation. The parties of the Left had agreed that, once in power, they would suppress the fascist leagues (such as the Croix de Feu and others). There would be a law obliging newspaper proprietors to disclose the source of any subsidies received. A national unemployment fund would be created; working hours were to be reduced without any reduction in wages; agricultural prices would be revalued upwards, but without any increase in the prices paid by the consumers. Finally, there was to be a tax reform with the object of putting an end to tax evasion by the leisured classes. The elections of May 1936 duly brought the Popular Front to power, or to be more accurate, the Socialists and the Radicals—the Communists having decided to support the government in Parliament, but without participating in it.

As leader of the SFIO (as the Socialist Party styled itself), Léon Blum was thus in power. His government's programme was closely based on that of the Popular Rally of the previous January. This was not exactly going to be 'socialism', since the Radicals had made it clear that they wanted none of it. However, it certainly meant a pretty strong dose of social reforms. Legislation was introduced for the 40-hour working week, for the nationalisation of the Bank of France, for the suppression of the fascist groups, for State control of the arms industry, for compulsory arbitration in industrial conflicts, and for paid holidays. All these laws were pushed through during the first few months. The domestic situation favoured reforms, the advent of the popular government having been accompanied by a huge wave of strikes and factory sit-ins. The international climate on the other hand, could hardly have been worse. In March shortly after the French elections, Hitler had occupied the Rhineland, after denouncing the Locarno Agreements. In May Mussolini's armies occupied Addis Ababa, thus completing the conquest of Ethiopia by fascist Italy. The immediate outcome was the collapse of the League of Nations, which had shown itself to be impotent in the face of aggression from the dictators. Finally, on 17 July 1936, civil war broke out in Spain.

With some reason, Blum feared a general war in Europe. He drew attacks from the Communists, led by Maurice Thorez, for receiving Dr Schacht, Director of the Reichsbank. Under strong pressure from the British and from his own Radicals the Prime Minister signed the Non-intervention Pact in the Spanish War, which meant that Britain and France would refrain from providing arms for the government of the Spanish Republic, whereas Germany and Italy had no such scruples in providing weapons for the nationalist insurgents of General Francisco Franco. It is true, however, that the government allowed the Soviet Union to use French port facilities to provide weapons for the Republic.

There was no shortage of internal problems as well, and these problems were exacerbated by the international situation: prices were rocketing; the franc was devalued in October 1936; the gold reserves, which had been satisfactory at the start, were dropping with a quite disconcerting speed. What was to be done? In March 1937 Blum announced a 'pause' in the reform programme, in the hope of reassuring the big companies and facilitating the floating of large-scale loans for national defence.

The mandate of the Popular Front was nearing its end. On 19 June the Senate turned down Blum's request for special fiscal powers. This brought down his government. The socialistic experiment had lasted less than a year. The Socialists came back to power in 1938 but lasted barely one month (13 March–10 April). Blocked once more by the Senate, Léon Blum resigned for the second time. As in England in 1923 and again in 1929, the Socialists in power had presented the spectacle of weak men incapable of coping with events, or of finding in the socialist texts any valid solution to the real problems of their respective countries.

In Spain the British and French experiences were confirmed, but to a worse degree. The Seventh Congress of the Comintern had dealt extensively with Spanish problems. Close attention was paid to the causes of the failure of the revolution of the Asturian miners in 1934, who had been crushed by Franco on the orders of the Centre-Right government of the Republic, and the Premiership of the radical leader, Alejandro Lerroux. What is certain is that the Congress confirmed the plans of international communism to seize control of the Spanish Revolution, which was judged to be imminent.

At the elections of February 1936 the new *Frente Popular* won a crushing parliamentary victory. It was not, however, the Front as such that came to power, but a Centre-Left coalition under the Premiership of the reformist and anti-clerical intellectual, Manuel Azaña. The Socialists and Communists had voluntarily stayed out of the government.

Already at that time Spain had become practically ungovernable, and was sinking ever faster into anarchy and violence. There were street fights, not only between the Communists and the Fascists of José Antonio Primo de Rivera, but even between the two main factions of the Socialist Party: the moderates under Indalecio Prieto and the revolutionists of Largo Caballero. The latter, aged 67, had been jailed for his part in the events of 1934 and had taken advantage of it to read Marx and Lenin for the first time. The Communists had awarded him the title of 'the Lenin of Spain'—of which he was inordinately proud. He preached revolution in terms of such violence that the bourgeoisie was terrified on hearing itself almost daily threatened with annihilation.

The Communists, although officially they supported the Popular Front, systematically spread the idea that Azaña would be the Kerensky of the revolution, destined to make room, when the time came, for 'the Lenin of Spain'. Their instrument in disseminating this notion was the crypto-communist Alvarez del Vayo, who belonged to the revolutionary faction of the Socialist Party. Curiously unmoved in the midst of growing disorder, Azaña was pursuing his own revolution. With an optimism that was scarcely believable in the orgy of rioting, strikes, murders and arson then ravaging Spain, he re-distributed land among thousands of peasants in the province of Estremadura. A tiny quota of socialism, nothing more.

In the shadows, the Army started plotting and organising itself. On 13 July at dawn, assault guards in uniform called at the home of the right-wing parliamentary leader Calvo Sotelo. They seized him from his bed, murdered him in a police vehicle, then dropped his body in a cemetery. Four days later Franco and his military colleagues took arms against the Republic. It was the start of the Spanish Civil War.

Henceforth, the war had a distorting effect on politics. There is no point in following the Popular Front in its increasing decadence in the hands of the Communists and the Anarchists.[3] It seems more relevant to note that the defeat of the Republic and the victory of the Nationalists, contrary to received opinion, by no means meant the end of socialism in Spain. On the contrary, Franco's economic policy between the end of the Spanish War and 1957 was objectively a *socialist* policy, despite the fact that the Socialist Party (PSOE) and the Communist Party were both banned (as indeed were all other parties) and their leaders were either in exile or had gone underground. Names and terms do not alter reality. All proportions kept, the Hitler–Mussolini phenomenon was being reproduced. In marked contrast to the German and Italian dictators, Franco was in no sense an ideologist. Two simple ideas dominated his thinking: the fatherland and a passion for order. He had served the Republic when it had given him the mission of restoring order in 1934. He had risen against it when it became painfully clear that it was going to allow the country to sink into disorder.

In substance Franco had become the leader of a *de facto* coalition of interests and tendencies: monarchists, business, the greater part of the Church and finally the Falange. This *Falange Española*, led by the son of the old dictator Miguel Primo de Rivera, certainly had some points in common with Italian Fascism and even with National Socialism, but not many. In contrast with Hitler and Mussolini who were both atheists, José Antonio preached respect for the Church and the practice of the Catholic religion. What the three men had in common were nationalism and some economic ideas. Although not a Marxist, José Antonio was anti-capitalist and against the exploitation of the poorer classes. In this manner he was a socialist.

Imprisoned by the Republicans, then executed, José Antonio was not given a chance to play any part in Franquist Spain. However, a key role was that of Franco's brother-in-law, Ramón Serrano Súñer. One afternoon in 1937, while Serrano and Franco were taking a walk in the gardens of the Bishops' Palace in Salamanca, Serrano suggested that Franco should form a powerful ruling party. Franco took his advice. This was the start of a new party in which the original Falange was only one of the participating groups. The new party fused together the *Comunión Tradicionalista* (Carlist Monarchists), the *Falange Española* and another fascist-type group, the *Juntas Ofensivas Nacional-Sindicalistas* or JONS. Inevitably, the new party was given a complicated name, *Falange Española Tradicionalista y de las JONS* (shorted to FET). In my biography of Franco I asked the question: 'A Fascist Party?' And my answer was: 'Yes and No.' Certainly it included the fascists. Yet it could equally be said that its creation condemned Spanish fascism to slow death by strangulation.

From 1941, during the Second World War in which Franco's Spain had managed to avoid participating, Franco, following Mussolini's example, created the *Instituto Nacional de Industria* (INI). For a Director, he turned to an anti-Republican industrialist, Juan Antonio Suanzes. This was the start of a 'State capitalism', which it was hard indeed to distinguish from socialism. In mid-1950 the INI already owned seventy enterprises. That same year the *Instituto Nacional de*

Colonización, recently created, bought back 296 properties that had been abandoned, and settled 23,517 peasant farmers on them. That too was socialism, curiously similar to the re-distribution of land in Estremadura undertaken by Azaña's Popular Front.

The so-called 'vertical' trades unions (*sindicatos*) brought together the representatives of the workers, the bosses and the government. They were certainly of fascist inspiration. The right to strike was denied to the workers. On the other hand they enjoyed exceptional privileges which many trades unionists in the democracies might well envy: special hospitals, luxurious holiday camps, social security, etc. And that too was socialism.

During its first phase Franquist socialism brought spectacular results. Spain's 'economic miracle' made a start: dams, factories and an autonomous automobile industry. However, from the mid-1950s this growth was accompanied by galloping inflation, a worrying rise in the external trade deficit, and a disastrous fall in the reserves of gold and hard currency, not to mention corruption and nepotism. Always the pragmatist, Franco in 1957 invited two teams of foreign specialists to Spain to look at the situation and give their advice. One came from the European Organisation for European Economic Cooperation (OEEC), the other from the International Monetary Fund (IMF). In 1961–62 he repeated the experiment in effect, bringing in experts of the Organisation for Economic Cooperation and Development (or OECD as the OEEC had been renamed), and from the International Bank for Reconstruction and Development, usually shortened to 'World Bank'.

Listening to this foreign advice the dictator decided to drop his Falangist ministers and appointed new technocrats, such as López Rodó, Ullastres and Navarro Rubio to the economic and financial posts. Apart from the *Sindicatos*, with their social and other privileges, these moves marked the end of the subsidised economy and the abandonment of Falangism and of *de facto* socialism. On the other hand, the enormous State investment in tourism turned out to be exceedingly profitable. The Spanish miracle now really blossomed. Towards the end of the 1960s Franquist Spain could boast the freest economy in Europe—that is, the one with the largest private sector. The dose of socialism had been excessive; but the advantage of being a dictator lies in the fact that it is relatively easy to change direction.

NOTES

1 There are several comprehensive histories of socialism, to which readers who wish to pursue the matter are referred. Among them, in English, there is

G.D.H. Cole's monumental *History of Socialist Thought* (eight vols, 1952–9); and in French, *Histoire générale du socialisme*, published under the editorship of Jacques Droz in five volumes.

2 In his definitive study, *The Harvest of Sorrow: Soviet Collectisation and the Terror Famine* (Hutchinson, London, 1986), Robert Conquest reaches a figure exceeding fourteen million for the final toll.

3 See Brian Crozier, *Franco: A Biographical History* (London, 1967).

5

The Welfare State in Britain

Most people naturally assimilate Britain's Welfare State with the Labour Party in power. As far as the creation of it is concerned there is nothing wrong with this correlation, but there is a tendency to forget that at the earlier stages of dream and gestation, the Welfare State was the collective creation of Winston Churchill's coalition government.

Already, before the First World War, in his capacity as President of the Board of Trade in the government of David Lloyd-George, Churchill, with his characteristic vigour, had advocated social reforms in depth. He had called for shorter working hours for coal miners and for the introduction of a social insurance scheme, which in fact became law in the shape of the National Insurance Act in December 1911.

At the time, of course, Churchill was a member of Lloyd-George's Liberal Party, having quit the Conservatives whom he had joined initially. The Tories held this desertion against him for many years. During the 1930s their future leader, by now in the wilderness, never tired of warning the country against the threat of Hitlerite Germany, at a time when Neville Chamberlain's Conservative Party was doing its best to appease the Axis dictators. It was not until the fall of France and the heroic debacle of Dunkirk that the Conservatives, with Leo Amery to the fore, appealed to the old warrior (who was already 66) to take over from the defeated Chamberlain. In May 1940, at last, Churchill became Prime Minister.

Having lived through the great depression and mass unemployment the British people, in the mass, were ready for a hefty dose of socialism. Within the government there was unanimity: the Conservatives, Labour and Liberals all agreed. The time had come to put an end to the misery that had prevailed between the wars. Henceforth, poverty was to be abolished by the combined force of the law and the people's will.

The great architect of the Welfare State, in any case, was not a politician but an economist named William Beveridge, who had long specialised in problems of employment and unemployment. At the height of the war the Churchill government gave him an interesting job: he was asked to prepare a study, taking account of the fundamental economic resources of the country and of social conditions, with the aim of spreading the benefits of social insurance to the population as a whole, without any class distinctions. The outcome, which deserves the epithet 'epoch-making', was a White Paper entitled *Social Insurance and Allied Services* (published in 1942 and forever after known as the *Beveridge Report*). Thus was a Welfare State created, at least in embryo.

There was an irresistible wave of popular enthusiasm for 'welfare' when the war ended in May 1945. The great mass of demobbed soldiers were going to vote Labour, blaming the Tories for the hardships which they or their families had suffered before the war. Many of them reckoned this was that they had been fighting for. Burying Nazism was, of course, the job they had taken on, but the real point was to bury the 1930s. Because of Britain's party political system, Winston Churchill—although he had led the country to victory and was in no way responsible for the misery of the 1930s—was swept out of power in the elections of 5 July 1945. In came Labour on a landslide vote. At the time of the elections the Potsdam Conference was in session. Deeply wounded by the people's ingratitude, but dignified to the end, Churchill handed over to the somewhat dull Labour Party leader Clement Attlee, who had been his deputy in the wartime coalition. Socialism thus found itself in power.

But was it really socialism? Within the Labour Party the true socialist ideologists had reservations, for everything depended upon the definition of socialism, which was open to the most diverse interpretations. When all was said and done, everything rested on the famous Clause IV of the Labour Party's Constitution, calling for the 'socialisation of the means of production, distribution and exchange'. In the eyes of the 'moderate' leaders the less said about Clause IV the better, especially during election campaigns. For the purists, however, Clause IV was the real *raison d'être* of the Party, and they would never tire of sniping at the leadership for stopping short of full socialism.

There were enigmatic aspects of the personality of Clement Attlee, who now headed the first Labour government since 1929. Just what did he stand for? Was he a moderate or would he go all the way to real socialism? He was quite widely known, still, as 'Major' Attlee, from his rank during the First World War and, with his clipped military moustache, he looked the part. With his sober grey suits and his 'public schoolboy' voice, he also seemed typical of the upper middle class.

Indeed, he had been a pupil at Haileybury before going up to Oxford. In terms of persona he looked reassuring enough to the bourgeoisie. A lawyer's son, Attlee practised for some time at the Bar in London, before developing a veritable passion for social reform. Between 1907 and 1922 (not counting his military service), Attlee lived in Stepney, one of the poorest areas of London's East End. As if to demonstrate his political leanings he became a member of the Fabian Society and the following year (1908), joined the Independent Labour Party, which was smaller but much more 'ideological' than the main one. After the First World War he became Mayor of Stepney, and three years later entered Parliament as MP for the neigbouring district of Limehouse.

Today, with the advantage of hindsight, it is clear that within the limits of legality, Attlee was really a kind of revolutionary. Certainly, he and his government profoundly transformed British society. Indeed he left his mark equally on foreign as well as on domestic affairs. During the war Churchill had said that he had not become Prime Minister to preside over the dissolution of the British Empire. History enabled him to keep his word although not in the way he would have wished, since when the time came to consider the future of the Empire he was no longer in power. It fell to Attlee to 'preside over the dissolution' of Britain's overseas possessions, starting with the brightest jewel in the Crown—India.

All this is background only. What really concerns us here is the internal policy of the Attlee government. The United Kingdom emerged from the war drained and exhausted. The sudden end of American Lend–Lease cast a heavy shadow over the prospects for economic recovery. On 6 December 1945 the United States, by now under the Presidency of Harry Truman (whom Attlee had met at Potsdam where Truman had succeeded the deceased Franklin D. Roosevelt) announced a massive loan to Britain of $3.75 billion. For the immediate future this was a necessary life belt, but for an exhausted country it was a heavy mortgage on the future.

Socialism could hardly have been launched in more unfortunate circumstances, but Attlee and his team were determined to keep their electoral promises. In February 1946 the government revived the trade union movement, which had been more or less paralysed during the later war years, by abrogating the emergency laws prohibiting strikes and the political activities of the trades unions. In fact, the Labour Party and the trades unions were inseparably linked: the money came from the unions, and political action from the party.

Between May and July 1945 socialistic measures came in abundance. Without delay the House of Commons approved the nationalisation of the coal mines, the extension of social insurance, State control over imperial communications and above all the creation of a National Health Service (NHS), designed to make the whole range of medical services available to the public 'free' (that is, paid for by taxes, which amounted to a transfer to income from the richer to the poorer).

Clearly, all this, and much more on the way was going to be expensive. Apart from coal and iron, the United Kingdom was poor in natural resources. Moreover, it had lost its traditional overseas markets, and there had been a heavy drain on investments abroad. Inevitably this was a time of severe shortages. In July bread and certain foodstuffs were rationed. It was worse than during the war. In January 1947 the nationalisation of the coal mines took effect in inauspicious circumstances; with a hard winter and a severe shortage of coal drastic restrictions on fuel and industrial production were initiated. Attlee's Minister of Fuel and Power, Hugh Gaitskell, future leader of the Labour Party, appealed to his fellow citizens to take only one bath a week and to use no more than five inches of water. He advised men to shave 'blind' to save on electricity.

Despite all this austerity the programme of socialisation went ahead. Between January and April the State took over all transport (railways, roads and canals) and electric power. The planning of villages and urban centres was brought under central control.

Britain's tiny Communist Party (CPGB) whose electoral attraction was feeble (although it did have two MPs in the Commons) took a jaundiced view of this rapid progress towards socialism, which seemed to make it look irrelevant. Despite its low electoral appeal the power of the Party was considerable through its acquisition of key posts in the trade union movement, although the general public was hardly aware of the situation. In January 1949 the Communists paralysed external trade with a general strike of the dockers. All ports were closed for two months, and Attlee decreed a state of emergency.

Thanks to the strike the foreign trade balance was even more in the red than it would have been. The pound was devalued—a dramatic fall from $4.03 to $2.80 and a fundamental shift from which sterling would never recover. Already in February 1946 the Bank of England had been nationalised, but State control over the bank of issue had no effect on the general economic situation. You pay cash for socialism.

The devaluation had been announced on 18 September 1949. With varying degrees of anxiety (or anticipation, as the case might be), many citizens started asking themselves just how far the Attlee government would go. In November a bill was introduced providing for the nationalisation of iron and steel. It was hotly contested in the Commons and barely scraped through the Lords. In any event no further action was taken on it until the second Attlee Parliament. To teach their lordships a lesson the government removed its veto on all legislation proposed by the Lower House. There was much indignation in the press and in Parliament but there was nothing to be done in the face of the crushing Labour majority.

Labour's mandate was, however, drawing to a close. In February 1950 Attlee decided to consult the voters. There were heavy Labour losses and the party's majority in Parliament fell from 148 to 7. Clement Attlee was still in No. 10 Downing Street but his situation had become precarious in the Palace of Westminster.

Moreover, the international situation hardly favoured any further extension of British socialism. Nowadays it is not easy to recall the attitude of the Attlee government towards international communism. Foreign policy, under the direction of Ernest Bevin, former boss of the huge Transport and General Workers' Union, was just as anti-communist as that of President Truman and his Secretary of State Dean Acheson. When the Korean War broke out in 1950 Britain lined up without hesitating at the side of the United States, within the framework of the United Nations.

A military commitment of this nature naturally implied a rearmament programme. On 29 January 1951, some weeks after the cessation of the Marshall Plan which provided economic aid to Britain and Europe, the Prime Minister announced an arms programme to be spread over three years, with a total expenditure of £4.7 billion. This was too much for some of Attlee's supporters to swallow. The most notable defector was Aneurin Bevan, possibly the best orator of his generation as his fellow-Welshman Lloyd-George had been in his. Bevan, the Health Minister, found it impossible to accept that armaments should be given any kind of priority over social services and resigned from the government. His departure caused a sensation. The son of a miner, a convinced socialist, Bevan was the true architect of the NHS. He had also presided over the large-scale plan for the construction of council dwellings under State patronage. Moreover, he was the Editor of the socialist weekly *Tribune*, which was, incidentally, always an open platform for the famous anti-totalist socialist George Orwell. Attlee would have preferred to keep this redoubtable personality on the government benches rather than give him the freedom to criticise his former colleague from the back ones.

As for socialism, it was now definitely relegated to second position, although the steel industry, the nationalisation of which had been decided by the first Attlee government, was brought under national control around this time. It was of course to be denationalised by future Conservative governments and then re-nationalised by Harold Wilson's Labour government of 1964–70. But this was truly the last convulsion of the socialisation programme. On 25 October, a fresh general election, which had become inevitable, gave the Conservatives a majority. Now aged 77, Winston Churchill was back in power.

Once established by the law, the Welfare State became part of the British way of life, along with the original dose of socialism. Except for the steel industry successive governments, whether Labour or Conservative, took good care not to interfere with it. Which is another way of saying that until the advent of Mrs Margaret Thatcher in 1979, the Conservative Party socialised itself without admitting it. There was indeed such a convergence between Gaitskell, the moderate Labour leader, and Mr R.A.B. ('Rab') Butler, the ideologist of neo-Conservatism, that the press coined a word for lexicographers to inherit: Butskellism. It was the Welfare State above all that was sacrosanct. The Conservatives, whether led by Churchill or Eden, by Macmillan or Heath, obviously took it as an unwritten rule that any party that showed the slightest sign, however timid, to tamper with the NHS would condemn itself to losing the next election. The Thatcher revolution, currently in full spate, has largely taken the form of 'privatisation' of industries formerly nationalised. But the hints occasionally dropped about the need to 'rationalise' (read 'reduce') the Welfare State was closely watched by the public as well as by the critics. The 'wets' (read 'social democrats') of the party, including the embittered ex-Prime Minister Edward Heath, had made their feelings crystal clear.

While in opposition during the 1950s, the Labour Party indulged, as parties in opposition often do, in a spot of introspection. Their object was to make some kind of a balance sheet of socialism after six years in power with the aim of planning for the future. This ideological task fell naturally to the party's great intellectual, C.A.R. Crosland, thinker and spokesman of the moderates, as distinct from Aneurin Bevan, the voice of the radical wing of the Labour Party.

'Tony' Crosland was generally considered as a gifted man with superior intelligence (of which he himself was not in doubt). Rather languid in gesture (perhaps because of the facility with which he mastered a brief and the problems that went with it), he lacked the iron will and the devouring ambition essential to the greatest political careers. After brilliant studies at Oxford, this scion of a good upper middle class family (like Attlee and other colleagues) decided, as so many others had done, to perform an act of penance for the collective sins of his class by joining the Labour Party. As a successful member of the Wilson Cabinet (Education, Trade), he was credited with the ambition of graduating in due course to Chancellor of the Exchequer and perhaps— who knows?—Prime Minister. Instead of which his political career reached its apex when he was appointed Foreign Secretary. He died suddenly, aged 59, in 1977.

His magnum opus, *The Future of Socialism*, came out in 1956, and was greeted with great critical enthusiasm, by no means confined to his fellow-socialists. In no sense a Marxist, Crosland was the apostle of the mixed economy, in which it would be sufficient for the State to control the 'commanding heights'. There was no question of destroying capitalism, but rather of redistributing the wealth created by the system. Crosland had noted in any case, and quite rightly, that capitalism, far from fading away or destroying itself, was in pretty good health.

The doctrine of full employment, of which he was a passionate champion, and of welfarism, rested upon an assumption which, in the first post-war years, seemed logical. Economic growth was taken for granted; this growth would automatically finance the ever-growing cost of the Welfare State.

Alas for the doctrine, the British economy—after a first spurt, which was hardly surprising since it was starting up again virtually from zero—began to falter during the 1960s. It was evident enough to objective observers that socialism was the reason. The nationalised industries were performing very badly and costing more and more money. The British people were losing the work habit, both because welfare cushioned them against unemployment and because incentives were inadequate. Indeed, what was the point of making an effort, since any additional margin in earnings was going to be absorbed in taxes? As for the unemployed, what was the point of looking for a job, since they and their families would be looked after by social security? As for the industrialists, with obvious exceptions, they too began to ask themselves what was the point of renewing their capital equipment, in the face of the hostile resistance to change and modernisation from the trades unions.

Despite the assumptions of John Maynard Keynes (and of Crosland himself) the Wilson and Heath governments had demonstrated a phenomenon which they were reluctant to recognise: that inflation and unemployment could go hand in hand. Inexorably Britain was tumbling in the chart of world economic performance, left behind not only by West Germany and Japan but even by France, which in 1955 had been considered the 'sick man of Europe'. From the third rank among the industrialised countries of the West, the United Kingdom fell quite fast to twelfth or thirteenth. In other words, the expectations of Labour's ideologist were simply not materialising.

In a brilliant article in *Encounter* in January 1977 ('Crosland Reconsidered') Colin Welch analysed Crosland's philosophy in depth and proposed a funeral oration: 'Mr Crosland was thus condemned to live in his own future. He saw it, and it didn't work.' Cruel, but accurate. British socialism had gone bust.

BOOK THREE

Everywhere a Failure

6

The Soviet Prototype

It is not enough to assert that socialism has 'failed' in the Soviet Union. One must also offer criteria upon which to judge success or failure, and the best criteria are surely those advanced by the revolutionaries who seized power in Russia in November 1917, eight months after the popular upheaval that had swept away the regime of the Tsars.

It is, of course, difficult to separate the 'socialism' practised by the Soviet Communist Party (CPSU) from the ghastly crimes committed by that party, but I shall make the attempt. I am not writing about the crimes of Soviet communism but about the economic and social performance of socialism in a country in which the ruling party had unlimited power to impose and administer socialism.

What, then, did the Bolshevik revolutionaries of 1917 claim or promise they were going to do in Russia?

Lenin was, of course, the leader of the Bolshevik revolutionaries and he made his own contribution to socialist theory, but the essentials of Lenin's programme had, in fact, been outlined seventy years earlier by Karl Marx and Friedrich Engels in *The Communist Manifesto* (see page 19). The *Manifesto*, published in 1848, called for the State ownership of the land, banks, industries and transport, the direction of labour, and the centralised control of education. In time, State communism (that is, socialism) would yield to a stateless communism of economic abundance—'from each according to his ability, to each according to his needs.' The State, Engels wrote with the naïve optimism of the true millennarian, would 'wither away'.

Let us return later to the communist view of the State. For now, I note only that socialism was supposed to lead toward 'communism,' defined as a condition of universal abundance. None of the early Marxist prophets, Lenin included, named even an approximate date for the achievement of abundance. The closest any Soviet communist came to it was in 1961, when Nikita Khrushchev presented the programme of the 22nd Soviet Party Congress, which claimed that 'the threshold of communism' would be substantially reached by 1980. But 1980 has come and gone, and no more has been heard of the 1961 prediction, which was preposterous even by communist standards of accuracy.

In addition to this Utopian and unprovable vision of the future, the 22nd Congress programme made a number of specific claims that are worth recalling. One was that by 1970 Soviet industrial production would surpass the American figure for 1961. This was perhaps a relatively modest claim by millennarian standards, but the programme went further by claiming that by 1970, the Soviet Union's industrial output *per head of the population* would surpass the American figure for the same year (1970). Again the stated year came and went and no official spokesman in the USSR was noticeably in a hurry to recall the predictions of so many years earlier.

Two years before the 22nd Party Congress, the ebullient Khrushchev had started the perilous habit of precise economic predictions, when he boasted in 1959 that by 1961, the Russians were going to produce more meat, butter and milk than the Americans. When the two years had elapsed, no more was heard of Khrushchev's boast. Indeed, by the end of Khrushchev's decade of power (1954–64), the American farmer still produced seven or eight times as much as his Soviet counterpart. In milk and livestock Soviet yields were only half those of America.

It would not be worth recalling these dead claims of the recent past were it not for the fact that at the time many commentators (by no means all of them communists or even socialists) took them seriously. I shall be bringing this dismal picture up to date, but for now let us return to Lenin. The main difference between, say, the programme of Britain's Labour Party today and the programme of the triumphant Bolsheviks between 1917 and 1921 is that the Bolsheviks actually carried theirs through, because the Tsarist State had collapsed; they had absolute power and were ruthless enough to use it.

The day after Lenin had seized power, that is, on 7 November 1917, a land decree was published ordering the immediate partition of large estates, the land to be distributed among the peasants—who were not told that they would soon be herded into collective farms. On 19 February 1918, the nationalisation of the land was proclaimed. When the civil war threatened the towns with starvation, the peasants were ordered to turn over their entire surplus to the government. When the peasants demurred, the government ordered forcible requisitioning.

As soon as they were in power, the Bolsheviks nationalised all the banks, confiscated private accounts, and repudiated the national debt. As early as 28 November 1917 the workers were given control of their factories. In theory the day of the soviets (workers' councils) had dawned. But again, as with the peasants, the workers were not told that it would not be long before the Party would take over from the soviets.

The reality was that the workers were ordered to join government-controlled trades unions and denied the right to strike (the argument—still in force, by the way, 70 years later—being that the workers would be striking against themselves, since they now owned their places of employment and the means of production). Compulsory labour followed, private trade was suppressed, and the government rationed the distribution of food and commodities.

The outcome of this first, and admittedly brutal, dose of socialism was that by early 1921, the world's first 'workers' State' was in total economic collapse. How did Lenin cure the economic ills created by his own brand of socialism? Certainly not by more rigorous socialist methods. Instead, in March 1921, he launched the famous, but short-lived, New Economic Policy (NEP), which, while it lasted, was a partial return to private enterprise.

The government stopped helping itself to the peasants' food surplus. Instead, a grain tax was introduced, which enabled them to keep some of the surplus for themselves. Freedom of trade within the country was reintroduced and a new land statute was passed (in 1922) to permit small individual farms and even the use of hired labour. Some small industrial plants were returned to their former owners, and private persons were allowed to start new enterprises. Private commercial establishments were also sanctioned in the cities, and the financial system was reorganised on a semi-capitalist basis.

All this did not amount to the abandonment of socialism, since large industry stayed nationalised and foreign trade remained a State monopoly. Even this relatively modest return to a market economy, however, produced dramatic results. The great famine of 1921 had been caused primarily by drought, but it was aggravated by the economic collapse caused by socialism. Under the NEP the national economy quickly sprang to life. In both industry and agriculture output reached the pre-war levels, and living standards, which had fallen drastically, recovered fast in town and country.

It is impossible to say whether Lenin would have drawn the obvious lesson from these circumstances (although one must assume that since he was a doctrinaire fanatic, he would have brushed them aside as an obstacle to his Utopian vision of the communist future). We shall never know for certain, since he died in January 1924.

During the next two years there was a power struggle between Stalin and Leon Trotsky, which Stalin won in 1926, when Trotsky was expelled from the party leadership.

As soon as Stalin had power in his own hands he set about resuming the discarded socialist programme and forcing the pace of socialisation. The period of the famous (or notorious) five-year plans began, on 1 October 1928. It is customary to date the Soviet Union's economic growth from that time, but some aspects of the situation are at times overlooked—such is the force of continuous propaganda.

The claim that it was Stalin's successive five-year plans that transformed the USSR from a backward peasant community to a great industrial power is partially true but in some respects a myth. For one thing Russia had been industrialising fast under the Tsars and had been a net exporter of grain. Of course, the country was devastated by war, revolution and civil war. But it took the Bolsheviks ten years in power (1917–27) to reach the level of production of 1914 Tsarist Russia.

The remarkable growth achieved under the five-year plans was almost entirely in the sphere of heavy industry. In other areas growth was small or nil. The systematic neglect of the consumer started at that time, but the real disaster area was agriculture. Stalin wrecked Russian agriculture, strictly in pursuance of communist dogma requiring the collectivisation of the land. In 1932 the harvest was lower than in 1927. By 1933 half the country's livestock had been slaughtered or had died for lack of feed. Twenty years later, when Stalin died in 1953, Soviet agriculture stood roughly where the Tsar had left it during World War One. Soviet citizens were eating less and their diet was less nutritious than it had been 25 years earlier. Yet the price for this colossal non-achievement was appalling: millions of peasants had been liquidated and millions more had been deported to the slave camps.

The obsession with heavy industry, which in effect has left the socialist fatherland far back in the race to abundance, needs a word of explanation. There were three reasons for this initial decision, rigorously maintained through the long decades of communist socialism. Two make sense of a kind; the third is difficult for non-communists to grasp, still less to accept as rational. The 'normal' reasons are these. Especially in the early days, the revolutionaries were building socialism for future generations to enjoy, and it was argued that the *Homo Sovieticus* of the future would enjoy the benefits of the fundamental capacity to be established in the first few years. The second reason was simply that it is far easier for a State-controlled economy to plan for heavy industry than for consumer industries. In a market economy the consumers largely determine supply through their own needs and demands. But under socialism the consumer economy has been abolished by decree and it is too bad for the consumer if the central planners decide that he or she needs pig iron and steel (which can be neither eaten nor worn).

The recondite third reason (which on reflection might even be the first in importance) was determined by Marxist doctrine. Marx had prophesied that the revolution would start in the most advanced industrialised countries. In fact it started in relatively backward peasant Russia. *Post facto*, therefore, it was decided that Russia had to be industrialised fast, to justify the Marxian prophecy. This curious aberration is explained more fully in Robert Conquest's introduction to the important book by the Yugoslav dissident Milovan Djilas, *The New Class*.

Under Stalin's forced industrialisation programme, the USSR became a formidable military power, as Hitler's hordes discovered. But the ordinary Soviet citizen's living standard remained pretty well static. The point is illustrated in the official Soviet statistics published in 1967 in anticipation of the fiftieth anniversary of the Bolshevik Revolution. On 15 September that year, the Communist Party organ, *Pravda*, proclaimed that between 1913 and 1967, total industrial production increased seventy-one times, whereas in the same period the output of light industry rose only seventeen times and of food production fourteen times.

As with all Soviet statistics, these figures are suspect, although there is no reason to doubt the proportions cited. In 1913, according to Western calculations, the average Russian could buy about 40 per cent of what the average American could buy. In 1967, the average American could buy five times as much with his money as his predecessor of 1913. If, however, the average Soviet citizen in 1967 had fourteen to seventeen times as much food and consumer goods at his disposal as in 1913, then one might conclude that in 1967 real wages had caught up with American level. But that was manifestly untrue. The fallacy is presumably a statistical one. In 1913 the bulk of the consumer goods available to Russians groaning under the Tsarist yoke came from the cottage industries, which are ignored by Soviet statisticians, who consider only Tsarist industrial output.

After 25 years of forced industrialisation under Stalin, living standards were no higher when he died than when he launched his first five-year plan in 1928. I am, of course, referring to the living standards of the ordinary Soviet citizen and his family. Those of the *nomenklatura*—the establishment—were incomparably higher, with town apartments and country dachas and access to foreign luxuries through special shops closed to outsiders (that is, to the bulk of the Soviet Union's population).

Even under Stalin's iron hand, however, the output of the consumer industries was becoming more sophisticated and ordinary people were beginning to develop a taste for 'consumer durables,' for cars, for washing machines, for cameras and watches. During the decades of terror and austerity, such hopes had been suppressed and the shoddy goods on offer were accepted because there was no choice. When Stalin died his designated successor, Georgi Malenkov, made speeches calling for a new deal for the consumer. Nikita Khrushchev, having got rid of Malenkov, partly on the pretext that such views were heretical, took over Malenkov's approach as his own.

The problem was that tastes and demand had become more sophisticated, but the factories were still turning out the old shoddy stuff. The result was the great inventory crisis of the late 1950s and early 1960s, when vast stocks of goods began to accumulate because few people wanted to buy them. Nothing could better illustrate the fundamental shortcomings of socialism than this phase of Soviet economic history, which is quite distinct from communist violations of human rights. Prices were fixed arbitrarily by the army of planners in Moscow who neither knew nor cared about the needs of the consumers. It was the planners who told the factories what and how much to produce. The planners fixed the production 'norms.' They might, for instance, decide that a particular year's target was 5 per cent more shoes, regardless of demand. There were penalties for failing to meet the norm and rewards for exceeding it. If vast quantities of shoes remained unsold that was too bad. The norm had been met, or exceeded, in the absence of a market mechanism to test the real demand for shoes.

It was in these circumstances that a private delivery system sprang up and grew rapidly;. It was, unfortunately, illegal, and the smart operator who made his profit by meeting the demand for consumer goods faced the penalties for unwanted success in a planned economy. In May 1961 Khrushchev extended the death penalty to various economic 'crimes': death to the freelance supplier.

In the early 1960s, a bold man started writing dangerously heretical articles, arguing that profits should be the index of the efficiency of an enterprise. His name was Yevsei Liberman. The word 'profits' sent shudders through the offices of Gosplan, the Soviet centralised planning agency. Professor Liberman, however, was clever enough to express his views in strictly ideological terms, with frequent quotations from Marx and Lenin and repeated definitions of 'socialist' profits, which were ploughed back into the people's enterprises, and thence into the pockets of the deserving workers and managers, as distinct from capitalist profits, which, of course, went straight into the pockets of capitalist exploiters.

Liberman's reward came in September 1965, when Premier Aleksei Kosygin made proposals incorporating some of Liberman's reformist ideas. In January 1966 a pilot scheme was launched, when 43 enterprises in 17 industries were brought into the 'profits' scheme. Each of the 43 had autonomy over its own show. By the end of 1968 more than 25,000 enterprises had switched to the reformed system. The results of this partial adoption of capitalist principles were gratifying. In 1966–67, industrial output rose by 20 per cent, and productivity by nearly 13 per cent.

Bold though the Liberman reform was, in its day, it could only be a palliative. It would have succeeded, in the full sense, only if socialist planning had been abandoned and the enterprises handed over to entrepreneurs. By definition, nothing of the kind could be envisaged, and the mountain of unsold goods began to accumulate again. Although big cuts in the prices of unsold goods were announced in April 1975, by October the total value of such stocks was estimated at 4.5 billion rubles, equal to about 2 per cent of the total retail trade. Simultaneously, private savings were rising dramatically. During the period of the five-year plan launched in 1971, under Leonid Brezhnev, the *increase* in private savings amounted to nearly 70 per cent of accumulated savings. Why were Soviet citizens saving so much of their incomes? One reason, of course, was that the incomes had risen. But the main reason was undoubtedly that they did not wish to buy the goods available in the shops.

It was in 1975, the last year of the 1971 plan, that an alarming new trend began. In the first six months of 1975 the USSR quite suddenly, after a relatively good year, developed a phenomenal trade deficit of $1.4 billion with the West. This reflected a fall of 3.5 per cent in Soviet exports to the West in the face of a rise of no less than 90 per cent in imports from the same countries.

This new situation was itself the outcome of the policy of 'détente' inaugurated by Brezhnev, whose advisers had persuaded him that the only way to draw level with and even overtake the United States in strategic military power, without too drastic a fall in Soviet living standards, was by making overtures to the West and attracting Western loans and credits on easy terms.

In the short term, at least, this policy was enormously successful. Western governments fell over each other in their eagerness to transfer high technology to the USSR, and Western banks competed in the provision of money to enable the Soviets to pay for what they were getting. By the end of 1981, the net indebtedness of the USSR to Western banks had reached $19.5 billion (44 per cent higher than for 1980)—yet another indication of the long-term failure of Soviet socialism in comparison with the 'doomed' capitalist system.

Another sign of long-term socialist failure had come some years earlier, with the signature on 20 October 1975 of a five-year grain deal between the USSR and the United States, under which the Soviets committed themselves to buying at least six million metric tons of American grain between 1 October 1976 and 30 September 1981. The significance of this contract lay in its tacit recognition that the Soviet leaders were no longer merely worried by the problem of an occasional poor harvest but by the continuing inability of the Soviet agricultural system to feed the population—after nearly sixty years of socialism.

In November 1982, the Soviet Union celebrated the sixty-fifth anniversary of the Bolshevik Revolution. There were slogans aplenty, including 'Glory to the CPSU' and 'We shall fulfil the 11th Five-Year Plan.' But the reality was that, according to Soviet statistics, labour productivity was *still* only 40 per cent of the American level.[1] Moreover, the USSR was no longer even catching up. During the first nine months of 1982, labour productivity had risen by only 8.3 per cent over the same period in 1981. In certain key sectors (oil, iron and steel, nonferrous metals, meat, and the dairy industry), productivity had actually fallen.[2]

It was the same old story. Soviet inventors had developed advanced automation systems. But the socialist planners had not found a way to mass-produce them. While the State Planning Committee and the Gas Ministry argued the toss, the oil and gas industry (to give an important example) was starved of advanced drilling equipment. That was Soviet socialism, 65 years after Lenin's coup.

It was also, of course, the inheritance of Yuri Andropov, the former head of the KGB, who took over as Party boss after the death of Brezhnev on 10 November 1982. I am not concerned here with Kremlinology, that abstruse semi-science which attempts, on inadequate evidence, to assess the changing balance of power within the top Soviet leadership. The point that interests us is the economic legacy, and the prevalence of corruption, and what, if anything, Andropov wanted or was able to do about these twin problems of Soviet socialist society.

The evidence of Andropov's period in power suggests that the answer was 'not much'. A lot of small fry were sacked or tried for minor corruption, such as the diversion of goods trains for the private sale of the goods being carried. But not much happened at the top.

The real problem was the economic system—in one word, socialism. In speeches and carefully leaked asides, Andropov let it be known that he was determined to modernise the economy, but even if his intentions were genuine he was up against the accumulated inertia of decades. At 69, and apparently in poor health, it seemed doubtful whether he would muster enough energy to do more than tinker with the system.

In August 1983 a report prepared some four months earlier for the Kremlin leadership found its way into the Western press (*International*

Herald Tribune, 4 August 1983). It called for a fundamental reform of the Soviet economy and asserted that its centralised management system could no longer ensure the 'full and effective use of the society's intellectual and labor resources'.

As *The Economist* pointed out that week (6 August), Andropov's experiment in 'reform', to date, was confined to two national ministries (out of more than 60), plus three smallish regions. The paper added: 'Now the staleness has started to creep back.'

Andropov died on 9 February 1984. After the customary grandiose funeral, he was succeeded by Konstantin Chernenko, who like him was an old man (73) and a sick one (in Chernenko's case, emphysema). Immobilism resumed.

A year later, Chernenko died in his turn, without having accomplished anything much. His death, however, did mark a turning point: the end of the era of the septuagenarians. He was succeeded by Andropov's protégé, the 'young,' 'dynamic,' 'intelligent' Mikhail Gorbachev, to use the fashionable epithets of the media.

The style had changed; this was immediately visible. As regards the substance, immobilism was still going to be the key word. On 12 June 1985, the new Party boss made an extremely severe speech in which he drew up a list of the ailments of the Soviet economy and specifically denounced three ministers who were responsible respectively for agricultural machinery, building, and steel.

As regards remedies, however, Gorbachev showed that he was no more flexible than the old men who had preceded him. He declared that it was necessary to modernise the economy, to motivate people by 'changing their attitudes towards work, stimulating quality by wage rises, and encouraging initiative on the part of the heads of enterprises'. In the same breath, he spoke of 'increasing the independence of enterprises' and of 'strengthening democratic centralism'. In other words, to attack the illness he was proposing to strengthen its cause.

In the absence of the self-correcting mechanism of the market, acute shortages of consumer goods were to be corrected by decree and the removal of incompetent officials. A Politburo announcement, published in all Soviet newspapers on 20 September 1985, called for an increase of at least 30 per cent in manufactured goods in the next five-year plan, from 1986 to 1990. The Soviet press, which can be surprisingly critical within approved guidelines, had been full of complaints about defective goods. *Izvestiya*, the government daily, had actually conducted an investigative report, of a kind familiar to Western readers, on the 'long queues and bare shelves of Moscow shops'. Not only were household goods in short supply, but even fruit and vegetables were scarce. *Izvestiya*'s reporters looked in vain for seasonal melons, peppers, and tomatoes, but found only shop after shop with a few dried-up apples. 'Want to see something surprising?' asked the newspaper scathingly. 'Go and look at one of our vegetable shops selling nothing but canned Bulgarian apricots.'

There was a striking contrast between Gorbachev and the aged Chinese leader Deng Xiaoping, and indeed between the USSR and the Chinese People's Republic. With Mao out of the way, the Chinese dared to think the unthinkable and say the unsayable: socialism was simply not working. It was going to be necessary, therefore, to indulge in a spot of capitalism, however modestly, for a start. In the Soviet Union, on the contrary, not only was it impossible to abandon the doctrine (the only source of legitimacy), but it was even apparently out of the question to experiment with methods borrowed from that permanent target of hatred, capitalism. In 1921 Lenin had launched his New Economic Policy; all Gorbachev could do was to threaten, or to encourage, according to circumstances. The system itself was to be left intact.

Is Soviet socialism curable, in this perspective? This seems to me rather improbable. For it is hardly possible to cure a system of socialism while remaining socialist. And the little handful of men in power in the Kremlin are well aware that they cannot discard socialism and stay in power. That is the real dilemma of communist regimes.

NOTES

1 *SSR v tsifrakh v 1980 godu* (Moscow, 1981), p.60.
2 *Ekonomicheskaya Gazeta*, No. 44 (October 1982).

7

Socialism in Eastern Europe

Stalin imposed socialism on Eastern Europe by force of arms and political coercion. The Soviet dictator's economic ideas were, perhaps, rather primitive. He believed in autarky—self-sufficiency. Each satellite economy was to be a carbon copy of the Soviet original, with most of the investment going into heavy industry, while agriculture and the unfortunate consumer were neglected. In Khrushchev's day, a more sophisticated approach began. Autarky yielded to the 'international division of labour'. In other words, each country in the Soviet bloc was supposed to concentrate on whatever it could do best, to the benefit of the bloc as a whole, and of the Soviet Union in particular. The Soviet and satellite economic plans were co–ordinated through a body known as Comecon, but whose real name is the Council for Mutual Economic Aid.

As in the previous chapter, I am not concerned here with communist repression, although it can never be entirely ignored. Undoubtedly political repression contributed to political dissatisfaction in Russia's East European dependencies. Without it the shortages caused by socialist planning might have been borne more patiently by the people. And there was another important factor: the natural resentment of formerly independent nations against the colonial power.

At all events, the only uses of military power in Europe since World War Two have been in Eastern Europe: The Soviet armed forces intervened in East Berlin in 1953 to suppress a workers' uprising; in Hungary in 1956; and in Czechoslovakia in 1968. Our concern here, however, is with the economic failure of socialism in all the countries of Eastern Europe without exception—the differences between them being of degree rather than kind.

Leaving aside the curious case of Albania which has followed its own course, and for some years was under Chinese, not Soviet, influence, there are also two other exceptional cases to consider. One is Yugoslavia—the only country of Eastern Europe in which communism was imposed not by the advancing Soviet armies but by the victory of communist guerrilla forces commanded by a Croatian leader whose real name was Josip Broz, but who was better known as Tito. The other exception to the rule of universal Soviet domination has been Romania, which under its dictator Nicolae Ceausescu has managed to assert some independence in international affairs, while sticking to a strictly Stalinist repressive regime at home. The point that interests us here, however, is that in Yugoslavia, as in Romania, the economic system has to be described as socialist.

There are people who doubt whether the Yugoslav economic system may correctly be so described. I am not among the doubters. Indeed Yugoslavia's official name is the Socialist Federated Republic of Yugoslavia. And the single ruling party describes itself, after several name changes, as the League of Communists of Yugoslavia. The differences between the Yugoslav system and all other regimes of Eastern Europe are nevertheless substantial.

Socialist planning is less rigid in Yugoslavia than elsewhere. The basic principle is sometimes described as 'planned guidance'. There is a plan, but the State does not directly administer the various economic enterprises. There is a fair amount of local autonomy, with a worker-management system in the factories, and co-operatives instead of rigid 'collectives' in agriculture. There is a free market for agricultural products and limited private enterprise on a self-management basis.

From a strictly Marxist standpoint, the Yugoslav economy is thus full of contradictions. One of the most paradoxical aspects of it, from a Soviet standpoint, is the fact that under Tito and his successors Yugoslavia in effect exports its unemployment problem by encouraging hundreds of thousands of Yugoslav workers to seek employment in the richer European countries, notably West Germany and Switzerland. One must not allow such paradoxes to carry one too far in assessing the character of the Yugoslav experiment. Foreign visitors are often told that the workers in Yugoslavia 'own' the factories they work in. It is not difficult to disprove this assertion. All that is needed is to put the question: 'If the workers own the factories, can they sell them and pocket the proceeds?' In fact, they cannot.

When Tito had his celebrated quarrel with Stalin in 1947–48, the Soviet dictator withdrew his hordes of advisers from Yugoslavia and Tito discarded the rigidities of Stalinist economics. As a result the prosperity in any given factory or enterprise is determined by that horrid capitalist word, *profit*. There is a fair amount of private enterprise, and foreign capital investment has been allowed since Tito decided to join the General Agreement on Tariffs and Trade (GATT) in 1966.

These innovations have diluted socialism, but without turning Yugoslavia into a capitalist country. Certainly the serious economic and financial crisis that came to a head in Yugoslavia in the summer of 1982 was remarkably similar to the simultaneous crises in other East European countries. It was a *socialist* crisis, not a capitalist one.

Tito died in May 1980, amid fears that the Soviet Union would attempt to reimpose its control over Yugoslavia now that its prestigious leader was out of the way. At the time of writing, Yugoslavia retains its independence. The economic crisis, however, had been building up while Tito was still alive. The extent of it became apparent when the League of Communists held its 12th Congress at the end of June 1982. There were heated debates on economic problems. The Prime Minister, Dušas Dragosavac, revealed in his main report that, at the end of 1981, Yugoslavia's hard currency debt stood at $20.1 billion. In 1982 alone, Yugoslavia had to find $5.3 billion worth of hard currency simply to pay the interest. The repayments were going to eat up 27 per cent of hard currency earnings of some $18.5 billion from exports, tourism, shipping, and the remittances of Yugoslavia's expatriate workers. Some weeks before the Congress a special law had been passed enabling the government to seize most of the foreign currency earnings which until then had been under the control of individual Yugoslav companies. According to *The World Today*, London, September 1982, of each $100 earned by an enterprise it could retain only $23.2.

Another speaker at the Congress, the new Foreign Trade Minister Milenko Bojanić, revealed that $1.7 billion less would be available for imports of raw materials and machinery than in the previous year. In the January–May period of 1981, industrial production had increased by 3.5 per cent; in 1982 during the same period, the increase was only 1.6 per cent. For the first time since the final break with the Soviet Union in 1948, when Yugoslavia's former allies had imposed a total economic blockade, industrial output had actually dropped—by 0.6 per cent. At the time of the Congress, many Yugoslav factories were sending their workers on compulsory leave. Some factories were going to close down permanently because of the shortage of hard currency for necessary imports. And all this against a background of 800,000 unemployed in a total labour force of just under 6 million in the 'socialist' sector of the economy (13.3 per cent).

THE ROMANIAN EXCEPTION

Romania shares with Yugoslavia the distinction of being (though to a lesser degree) an exception to the rule of total subservience to Moscow.

But in economic terms the two countries are poles apart. Yugoslavia has diluted its socialism; Romania has stuck rigidly to the unimaginative original Stalinist model. The contrast between the two countries, indeed, provides a perfect illustration to my 'second Universal Rule of socialism': The more there is of it, the worse the failure.*

The relative independence of Romania in international affairs is usually associated with the personality of Ceausescu, but his pre-decessor, Gheorghe Gheorghiu-Dej, started the process. Khrushchev, moving away from Stalin's autarchy in favour of the 'international division of labour', had cast Romania in an agricultural role. Gheorghiu-Dej did not like this at all. As a small-scale carbon copy of the USSR, Romania had had a taste of industrialisation and wanted more of it. Khrushchev called a meeting of Comecon to discuss his ideas for supra-national planning. Unexpectedly, the Romanian delegates declared that they would not accept supranational planning. They were not against some co-ordination of national plans, but individual national interests had to be respected.

In mid-1963, the Soviets summoned the economic leaders of all member-states of Comecon to Moscow to discuss Romania's hostility to supranational planning. The Romanians dug their heels in and got their own way. By the time the next full meeting was held, in Prague at the end of January 1965, the East European power grid had been extended to Romania, a common pool of railway freight cars had been set up and a joint oil pipeline completed.

Thereupon, Gheorghiu-Dej died, and Ceausescu stepped into his shoes on 22 March 1965. He continued to resist any attempts by Comecon to impose its rule upon his country. Instead he improved Romania's economic links with Western countries, encouraging Western tourists to visit Romania and contribute to its economic development with their expenditure of hard foreign currencies.

As time went on Ceausescu encouraged a 'cult of personality' to grow around him, the only rival of which in the communist world is the similar cult of the personality of the North Korean leader, Kim Il Sung. The political implications of this cult need not concern us here but it had unfortunate economic consequences. Western observers coined the term 'gigantomania' to describe some of Ceausescu's vast and unnecessarily ambitious projects, such as the construction of oil refineries with capacity three times as high as production would justify, and steel production facilities far in excess of Romania's capacity. Per capita, Romania by 1982 had become the second largest producer of steel in the world, next to the United States. Nobody knew quite what to

*   See Prologue, p. xii.

do with the new Navodari oil refinery, the original purpose of which was to process Iranian crude oil for the European market. Nobody had the courage to call for a halt in the construction of a deep canal from the Danube to the Black Sea—a high-cost scheme that looked as though it would be useless if European oil imports continued to be reduced by the search for alternative sources of energy. For all the expensive promotion, tourism proved an expensive flop. By mid-1982 a catastrophic shortage of basic foodstuffs had developed. Bread, flour, potatoes, green vegetables, cooking fats, and meats had all but vanished. Even corn-flour, which at one time was to be found in even the poorest households, had disappeared. Even for a Balkan country corruption and the black market had reached unprecedented levels, and all efforts to control them through rationing and draconian controls had failed. The plan was disastrously underfulfilled, and the harvest shortfall was nearly one-third.

Statistics made the economic picture look rosier than it really was. For instance, between 1950 and 1981, per capita income rose from $100 to $1,500, but the standard of living had not increased proportionately. In the 17 years to 1982, industrial production had risen on average 11.4 per cent a year, and five million new jobs had been created in industry since 1950. But the hard reality was that the government had cut the military budget by 10 per cent and was reduced to rationing private driving to alternate days, despite interminable waiting queues at service stations.

As usual with a member of what Brezhnev called the 'Socialist Commonwealth', Romania in the depth of its economic crisis turned to the West for help. By the end of 1981 Romania's foreign debt had reached $9.6 billion—5.5 per cent up on the previous year—and by the end of 1982 Romania was in arrears on its international payments. As with other East European countries, Ceausescu asked the International Monetary Fund for a rescue loan—in his case for $300 million. As usual with applicants for IMF loans, President Ceausescu was told to cut the growth of domestic spending, reduce imports, and initiate various reforms. To this, his response was to dismiss his Prime Minister, Ilie Verdet, eight deputy premiers, and several members of the Political Executive Committee. Whether Romania's economy was capable of reforming itself under Ceausescu's rigidly ideological rule remained an open question.

THE REST

It is perhaps even more difficult to distinguish between communism and socialism in Eastern Europe than in the USSR itself. For Eastern

Europe is, in the strictest sense, a colonial area. Stalin imposed Soviet-style communism on the 'liberated' countries of Eastern Europe by force and guile. With communist one-party rule came integral socialist economies. The local peoples had not asked for either. They got both.

East Germany is perhaps the most interesting case of all, because of the division of Germany, so that for 15 years or so it was possible to compare 'capitalism' in West Germany with socialism in East Germany.

Germany as a whole had been devastated, so that both systems started out pretty well from zero. To be fair, East Germany's handicap was to be even worse than West Germany's, in that the Soviets under Stalin looted the areas they occupied on a grand scale—in the guise of 'war reparations'. (I am not here concerned with the morality of what they did, in the light of the devastation inflicted on the USSR by Nazi aggression. I am simply recording what happened.)

In the West there was much doomsday talk, but relatively little action. In the East Stalin just got on with it, unburdened by scruples. President Roosevelt's Secretary of the Treasury and personal friend, Henry Morgenthau Jr., had called for the destruction of German industry and for the reduction of Germany to a pastoral economy. The Morgenthau Plan as it was called, came to nought, however. Roosevelt died and Morgenthau resigned shortly after his death.

In the East Soviet looting really was on a grand scale. During the brief period when the Red Army was in sole occupation of Berlin, the Soviets removed 75 per cent of all capital equipment. In those few months, machinery from some 1,900 industrial enterprises in the Soviet occupation zone was dismantled and shipped to Russia. It has been estimated that reparations to the Soviet Union in the postwar period amounted to 66.4 billion marks. Under Stalin's orders, all the industrial properties of 'war criminals,' National Socialists (Nazis), and militarists were expropriated. In effect private enterprise was simply eliminated from all large and most medium-sized industrial firms.

Stalin had hoped to extend 'socialism' to the whole of Germany, but nevertheless went easy over socialising measures in the Soviet occupation zone, seeking to reassure his wartime allies and persuade them to accept the reunification of Germany on his terms. It was not until the German Democratic Republic emerged in 1949 that the imposition of socialism really got under way.

One of the first things the East German regime did was to confiscate all privately owned farms of more than 100 hectares. Then years later—in 1959—about 52 per cent of the country's arable land had come under collective control. A new drive started in 1960 and by the end of the year, the regime could claim that agriculture was 98.7 per cent socialised. At the height of this drive, in one three-month period, about 340,000 farmers had been forced to join the co–operatives or had fled to the West.

The usual consequences followed. In 1969, the grain harvest dropped 12 per cent below that of the preceding year; there was a 30 per cent shortfall in potato and sugar beet crops. For years after 1964, East Germany was forced to buy more than one million tons of grain each year from the Soviet Union—until the Soviet Union itself ran into acute difficulties for exactly the same reason. Both East Germany and the Soviet Union thereupon started buying grain on a large scale from the capitalist United States.

Forced industrialisation on the Stalinist pattern created further economic difficulties for East Germany. As usual, centralised planning created anomalies. One whopping error was the construction of a huge steel combine at Stalinstadt which cost $600 million, yet proved unable to produce anything except crude pig iron. As with other East European countries, East Germany's development under socialism was hampered by the requirements of Comecon as a whole. For example, plans to develop Rostock as a major seaport and shipbuilding centre were suspended, because Comecon had decided that competition from Rostock could harm the Polish port of Szczecin (formerly Stettin). The aircraft industry was simply dropped. Textile plants and motor car factories were held back. On the other hand a giant uranium mining complex, employing 140,000 workers, was maintained at the Wismuth Aktiengesellschaft purely to provide for Soviet needs.

In striking contrast, once the Western Allies had given the job of Director of Economic Council for the Joint Anglo-American district to Dr Ludwig Erhard in 1948, the West German economy took off rapidly. Erhard believed in free enterprise and the market economy. He began by sweeping away most price and wage controls and by abolishing rationing. The socialist economists were scandalised, but he stood his ground. Almost overnight the factories were in production, the black markets vanished, and the shops were filled with goods. Within a year the national income in real terms was back to the 1936 level. There was a temporary increase in unemployment, which reached 11 per cent in 1950; but it then declined steadily to only 0.8 per cent in 1961. Erhard swept away rent controls and reduced income tax. Between 1949 and 1977, West Germany maintained the lowest inflation rate among industrial countries—only 2.7 per cent. This was the 'German miracle'.

In their millions East German men, women and children fled to the West, 'voting with their feet', as Lenin once said in a different context. Altogether, West Germany had to absorb some 14 million refugees.

Admittedly, many of these came from what had been East Germany—the lands absorbed by Poland in compensation for territory seized by Stalin under the Nazi-Soviet pact of 1939. However, East Germany was being bled white by the decision of nearly 30,000 citizens *every month* to leave their Socialist paradise and seek to better themselves under the booming economy of West Germany. To be sure, these dissatisfied East German citizens were also fleeing the rigours of communist repression. The point is that they preferred to drop everything, leave their homes, take themselves and their families to capitalist West Germany. To stem the flow, Khrushchev (who had succeeded Stalin) built the Berlin Wall—a hideous line of concrete and barbed wire with lethal devices to keep the citizens of East Germany within its borders. Despite this stemming of the drain of East German brain and skills, the growth rate of the East German economy declined after the building of the wall.

If the regime's statistics are to be believed, growth had reached the exceptional figure of 12 per cent in 1959, and the East German leaders were emboldened to prophesy that by 1961 they would surpass West Germany in per capita production. But the growth rate declined to 8 per cent in 1960, then to 6.2 per cent during 1961, settling down thereafter to an average of about 6 per cent. Needless to say the East German regime did not overtake the performance of the German Federal Republic. A further boast that it would do so by 1975 also failed to materialise. It is interesting to note, nevertheless, that the well-known qualities of the German people—in hard work and organisation—did assert themselves in East as well as West Germany, so that the East Germans—in spite of socialism—achieved the highest living standards in the Soviet bloc and became the tenth industrial power in the world.

In each of the East European upheavals (including Poland in the 1980s), economic as well as political factors played a part. In East Berlin and in Hungary, for instance, the workers had been growing more and more fed up because of the system of workers' norms—that is, quotas of work—which had been imposed in the factories. Every so often norms were raised, which automatically reduced the wages of the majority of the workers. As I said earlier, it is not easy to distinguish between communism and socialism in these matters. Obviously the decision to raise norms was a political one. But one of the purposes was to screw more output out of the workers—an economic purpose. From the workers' point of view the effect was economic. They felt they were being made poorer and poorer. Ironically it was under communism that the workers were being 'pauperised'—whereas Karl Marx had forecast the pauperisation of the workers under capitalism. Then the workers, having had enough of this new form of exploitation, started rioting in the streets; and that was a *political* action on their part.

More purely economic factors played their part in the upheavals in Czechoslovakia and Poland, although it would be wrong to exaggerate their importance in comparison with resentment at the injustices of arbitrary rule.

There is a monotonous sameness about the economic ills of the 'Socialist Commonwealth'—understandably, since they stem from the same causes. In happier times the economy of Czechoslovakia had been relatively advanced and well-balanced. Then came centralised planning and the usual zeal for large-scale production of capital goods. The result, by the mid-1960s, was a superficially impressive economic boom which went on for about a decade. It was a defective boom, for while heavy industry was growing, light industry, consumer goods and agriculture were declining fast.

By 1963, there was a serious recession. Czech technology—at one time well able to hold its own with that of the West—started dropping well behind. The 'Prague Spring' of 1968 was a revolt of the intellectuals, and of a part of the Communist Party itself, against local oppression and subservience to Moscow. But a stagnant and unbalanced economy made its contribution to the gathering ferment.

There is an interesting contrast between the economic policies of Hungary and of Czechoslovakia after their respective upheavals. The Hungarian approach was certainly the more enlightened. After the brutal and bloody repression of 1956 the government of Janos Kádár gradually relaxed the rigours of communist rule, both politically and economically. In agriculture—there as elsewhere in the bloc a disaster area—incentives for the farmers were increased so that by the late 1970s the country was again self-sufficient in food, as it had been before the war. In industry the regime decided to borrow heavily from the Yugoslavs, with a good deal of local autonomy for individual factories and the introduction of a market system for prices.

By mid-1970, the central planners had to a large extent surrendered their control. At the time of the failed revolution in 1956 they controlled something like one million prices. Fourteen or 15 years later, only a thousand prices were centrally determined. As a result, by all accounts, the atmosphere in Hungary was relatively relaxed and the Hungarians were more inclined to smile and laugh than their neighbours.

In Czechoslovakia, Gustav Husak, the austere party man who took over when the Soviets had deposed his hapless predecessor, Alexander Dubček, did make some material concessions, but seemed afraid of going too far along the Yugoslav path. In politics, incidentally, he made no concessions at all and the regime remained highly repressive. Some observers of the Czechoslovak scene described what happened as a kind of 'unwritten social contract': dreams of political reform were shelved, in return for greater material comforts. Personal consumption rose by 27 per cent during the 1971–75 plan period. Real wages rose by more than 5 per cent. The private automobile—that symbol of affluence— came into its own. In 1971 only one person in 17 owned a car. By 1975 it was one in ten, and in 1979 one in eight.

In Poland economic difficulties came in waves. On a number of occasions workers' riots caused political changes. The workers' riots in Poznan in June 1956 brought a change of party leadership four months later, when Wladyslaw Gomulka came to power. But Gomulka himself was forced to step down after similar riots in December 1970. His successor, Edward Gierek, promptly announced a 'new development strategy'. Capital and technology would be imported from the West, to be paid for by increased production in Poland itself. Instead, Poland found itself relying more and more on ever-growing Western credits, without any visible means of repaying debts thus contracted. In 1976 came more workers' riots. Four years or so later, generalised unrest led to the emergence of the independent trade union group calling itself Solidarity, which for a time competed with the officially sponsored trade unions.

In agriculture, incidentally, Poland was the exception to the communist rule. After the failed revolution of 1956, all serious attempts to collectivise agriculture were abandoned, so that about 70 per cent of Polish farms to this day remain in private hands. In principle this reliance on the private sector ought to have made a vast contribution to the agricultural sector. However, the ruling party retains full control of incentives, grain feed for cattle, and fertilisers. Individual farmers own the land they till, but have no control over their own destinies. The advantages of private farming thus have been largely denied to the country.

When the great oil crisis of 1973–74 hit the West, with the massive price increases decreed arbitrarily by the oil-producing countries' cartel known as OPEC, the regimes of Eastern Europe felt smugly protected. The USSR was their main supplier and the regimes of Comecon felt secure. A rude awakening was on its way. The Soviet Union increased its sales of oil to the West and simultaneously raised its prices for East European importers. By 1980 Czechoslovakia, for instance, was paying nearly five times as much per ton of Soviet oil as in 1970. The 'oil shock' of the late 1970s thus made its unwelcome contribution to the deepening economic crisis in Eastern Europe. Not one of the Comecon countries was able to meet its planned targets during the years 1976 to 1980. Most of them experienced severe food shortages. Poland and Romania

had been net exporters of grain but had to start importing it. Food rationing was introduced in both those countries. In 1981 East Germany's
grain imports from the United States cost some $370 million. One
outcome was drastic increases in food prices in the East European
countries. In Czechoslovakia, for instance, the price of meat had hardly
changed for two decades. Then, on 30 January 1982, the party decreed
a rise of 41 per cent. About the same time Romania raised the prices of
more than 200 food items by 35 per cent on average. In Poland the rise
was quite staggering: an average increase of 241 per cent in food prices
as a whole, decreed and announced on 1 February 1982.

A MOUNTAIN OF DEBT

Perhaps the most striking illustration of the inferiority of socialist
economics as compared with the economics of free enterprise and the
market, was the growing mountain of debt accumulated by the Eastern
bloc during the late 1970s and thereafter. The fact that certain important non-communist countries (such as Brazil, Mexico, and Venezuela)
were also seriously indebted to Western banks made no difference. It
was the socialist system as a whole that was in crisis and had turned to
the West for help—not the other way round. The communist theorists
were fond of talking about the supposed 'general crisis of capitalism'.
The reality was a general crisis of communism and its socialist
economic systems.

In June 1982 Comecon issued official figures for the level of debt of
its component members at the end of 1981. The overall figure was $80.7
billion. The net indebtedness to Western banks of the USSR itself was
shown as $19.5 billion (44 per cent higher than for 1980). Per capita,
Poland was well ahead: $24 billion (136 per cent up). The Hungarians
and Romanians had performed better, but only in comparison. Hungary
was regarded by Western academics as having the best-managed
economy in Eastern Europe, but that was not saying very much. The
Comecon figures showed an accumulated Hungarian debt of $7.8
billion for 1981 (54 per cent up on 1980). Romania's foreign debt stood
at $9.6 billion (5.5 per cent up on the previous year) and was rising
rapidly.

It is fair to note that during the same period the economies of the
major Western powers were in deep recession—the most severe of its
kind since the Great Depression of the 1930s. The point, however, is
that socialism was supposed to produce abundance, and to avoid the
recurrent crises of Western economic systems. Clearly, on the evidence
of the Eastern bloc's own economists and statisticians, it did
neither.

UNEMPLOYMENT DISGUISED

The socialist countries guarantee the right to work as fundamental. All of them, led by the USSR, boast that there is no unemployment in their countries, although it is high in Western Europe. In our Western capitals the defenders of socialism, even when they admit the sad reality of repression and misery in the countries of the Eastern bloc, tend to console themselves with a defensive reflex: 'At least,' they say, 'there is no unemployment in the socialist camp.'

The reality is quite different. There is unemployment all right in the countries of the socialist East, but it bears another name: 'social parasitism.' On 17 October 1984, the assistant attorney-general of the USSR, Nikolai Bazhenov, drew public attention to the phenomenon. Any individual without a job and without a fixed abode for more than four months is officially listed as a 'social parasite'. Such 'parasites' are charged, and since 1983 are automatically sentenced to one or two years in a labour camp—that is, in the gulag. According to Bazhenov 90,000 parasites were sentenced by the tribunals in 1983, and in September 1984 the police had 500,000 parasites on official file.

From the outside it is not easy to calculate the current population of the gulag. According to the Helsinki Monitoring Group (which manages to function more or less in the USSR in the face of police harassment), it is around 5.5 million. Some years ago a Congressional inquiry in the United States estimated the total at 4.5 million. It would be wrong to suppose, as many automatically assume, that most of the detainees are political dissidents. In fact they constitute a relatively small minority, the overwhelming majority being 'social parasites' (read 'unemployed'). According to a special report from the U.S. State Department, published in February 1983 under the title 'Forced Labor in the USSR', there are only around 10,000 dissidents in the gulag (on the other hand, the actual camps are very numerous: 1,100, according to the report). It is true that after the advent of Andropov as head of the KGB, official preference was given to 'curing' dissidents by injecting them with powerful drugs in psychiatric hospitals.

As always the satellite regimes take their cue from Moscow. Thus in Poland in 1983, 23,190 'parasites' were sentenced to forced labour. Among them and also in Czechoslovakia were opponents of the regime who had lost their jobs and were turned down by any potential employer because of their political record. This means that all dissidents given their conditional liberty remain unemployed because nobody dares offer them a job. Thus they soon qualify for a further sentence for 'parasitism'.

The French historian Jacques de Launay, after much research, estimated that unacknowledged unemployment probably reaches about 20 per cent of the working population in the countries of the socialist bloc. To this should be added a considerable measure of underemployment, for absenteeism averages between 15 and 21 days per person per year.

What are the causes of absenteeism on such a scale? They are many and varied: technical stoppages because of late deliveries of raw materials, or repairs to machinery; but also, birthdays and anniversaries, well-timed absences to join shopping queues, and personal economic activities (the labour black market). Such practices are widespread enough to lead to the employment of several people to do one person's job. Unfortunately it is not easy to measure under-employment. What is certain is that it constitutes a heavy burden on the socialist economies.

What is also certain is that socialism, in this domain as in others, does not offer a valid solution to the economic problems of the industrialised countries.

8

Far Eastern Models—and Cuba

In this book there is very little to be said about socialism in China, North Korea, and Vietnam—but rather more about Cuba. The reason why I have relatively little to say about the three Far Eastern countries is simple: in all three, the *communist* element, as distinct from that of *socialist* planning, was overwhelming. In all three, again, the irrational element of mad dictatorship was strong. All three were totalist tyrannies of the worst kind—worse than the USSR by my rule of thumb about such regimes: can the ordinary man or woman (that is, *not* members of the ruling party) opt out of politics? In the Soviet Union opting out is possible, up to a point. In China under Mao, opting out was virtually impossible—the ubiquitous street committees saw to that. If anything, North Korea is worse. As for Vietnam the message of recent visitors is that to some extent the inhabitants of Ho Chi Minh City (which used to by Saigon) can get away with a bit of freelancing on the side, by native wit and because the communists did not overrun this southern capital until 1975. North Vietnam, in contrast, has had full-scale communist control since 1954, and a good dose of subterranean communism since 1945, spreading gradually during the unhappy First Indochina War, involving the French.

In this group Cuba might seem the odd man out, and in a way it is. All four of the examples in this chapter, however, do have something in common: all three are, or were, peripheral countries in the great communist empire: China broke away; North Korea, under its own mad dictator, is not exactly a Soviet satellite; Vietnam is; and so is Cuba.

THE GREAT HELMSMAN

The leaders of communist countries tend to concentrate great powers in their hands, and to become the centre of a 'cult of personality'. They become gods. Their likenesses, on a gigantic scale, are displayed everywhere, in picture form or in sculpture.

Of no communist country was this truer than of the Chinese People's Republic. Such was the build-up of the personality of the leader of the Chinese Revolution, Mao Zedong, that the image of 'the Great Helmsman' (as he liked to be called) was accepted in countries that ought to have known better. (The sycophantic obits in the Western press when the Great Helmsman died in 1976 made nauseating reading.)

Whether he or Stalin was the greater mass murderer is difficult to determine. This is not, however, the aspect of Maoism that concerns us here. The reason why China under Mao does not have much to teach us about *socialism* in action is that on two separate occasions the Great Helmsman, in fulfilment of his private follies, utterly wrecked the Chinese economy.

The first occasion was in 1958, when Mao launched what he called the Great Leap Forward, from which the long-suffering Chinese fell flat on their faces. Until then, by the tenets of socialist planning in a relatively primitive economy, the Chinese Communists had not done too badly. They were producing quite a lot of steel—about three times as much as India when disaster struck—and by mobilising mass peasant labour they were doing pretty well with flood control and other desirable tasks. Moreover, although the agricultural performance was not brilliant, at least distribution had improved. The people were not among the best-fed in the world, but there was some substance to the official claim that famine had been abolished. Mass campaigns had virtually wiped out flies and sparrows, and disease was on the retreat.

Then Mao went haywire. Not for him the distant mirage of communism—abundance for all—the image of plenty that retreated just as you thought you were drawing near to it. Besides, he was tired of listening to the Russians, whose technicians in those days, swarmed over the vast country. He was going to bring in communism *now*, in his own lifetime.

In 1957 when this bold idea occurred to the great leader, China's population was already estimated at 600 million. This was 'the people' and there was nothing, but nothing, that 'the people' could not do in its collective genius. A tremendous unified effort, mobilising all 600 million hard-working Chinese, would at a bound carry the People's Republic forward over the threshold of 'communism', leaving Russia far behind.

Almost overnight, the 750,000 collective farms were merged into vast communes—26,000 of them—in which the individual would sink virtually without trace. The peasants ate in huge communal messes and the sexes were segregated in vast dormitories, with one room reserved for husbands and wives to get together at predetermined times for pro-creative duties.

But the greatest effort of all was to go into building, virtually over-night, a gigantic steel industry. All over the country workers and peasants were exhorted to build 'backyard furnaces'. As the year wore on (1958) the Party kept on raising production targets. Mao's approach was purely hysteria and mysticism. He had decided that China no longer needed scientists or technicians. The collective genius of 'the people' was all that was needed and the hapless scientists and technicians, together with 'intellectuals', were put to work in the fields. Fertiliser was short, but what did that matter?—each Chinese was his own fertiliser factory.

The final outcome, as might have been predicted, was economic dis-aster on an incredible scale. The rail system, already inadequate, had been totally disrupted through moving 'steel' from place to place. Food supplies became uncertain. To please the Great Helmsman local Party bosses had faked all production figures. A steel output of 11 million tons had been claimed. Now the shamefaced bosses admitted that not more than 8 million tons of the stuff was truly steel; the rest was unusable. A grain harvest of 375 million tons had been claimed. In 1959 it was admitted that the true figure did not exceed 250 million. And so on. In December 1958 Mao Zedong resigned as Chairman of the Republic (though he remained as chairman of the Communist Party).

The next great disaster Mao inflicted on the Chinese people started in 1966, and was termed the Great Proletarian Cultural Revolution. It lasted about four years and, as a man-made disaster, was even worse than the Great Leap Forward.

There is no space here to describe this period of madness, when young people were turned against their elders, encouraged to destroy as much of China's immemorial culture as they could, and to humiliate or actually kill members of the vast bureaucracy that held the country together.

Mao's purpose was to get rid of his rivals, especially the 'perfect com-munist', Liu Shaoqi, who had replaced him as chairman of the Republic, and the Central Committee's chairman, Deng Xiaoping. Deng in par-ticular was disgraced and Mao coined a choice insult for him: he was branded a 'capitalist roader'. But after Mao's death in 1976 Deng came back and gradually made himself the most powerful man in People's China.

He even proved, within limits, that Mao's insult fitted him, for in his attempt to bring some prosperity to the sorely tried Chinese people, he went so far as to encourage Chinese entrepreneurs from Hong Kong to build factories in South China and do business. Undoubtedly China today is a far more relaxed, less tormented country than it was under Mao. Less totalist too, in that it has even become possible to 'opt out' so long as one does not actively oppose the system.

Deng's reforms involved four areas: agriculture, industry, science and technology (counted as one) and defence. Central planning had not been abolished, but its range was now severely restricted. Henceforth the planners would focus on certain priorities, especially energy and raw materials. Agriculture in particular had been largely relieved of the dead hand of the bureaucrats. The peasants, minus the bureaucratic burden and in good heart, could now freely peddle their fruit and vegetables in the marketplace just as in the good old days. The people were eating better, as could be seen by all, and public health was improving as a result. As for the 'small' consumer goods, such as furniture or kitchen utensils, the producers were now left to decide what to manufacture to meet the demand of the market.

As for Hong Kong, the teeming population of this capitalist island on the edge of oriental communism is haunted by the fateful deadline of 1997, marking the definitive end of the era of British sovereignty. Britain had gone to war in 1982 to defend its sovereignty over the Falkland Islands, that is, to defend the freedom of fewer than 2,000 kith and kin threatened by the Argentine invaders. But there was never any question of holding the line in Hong Kong against the enormous mass of People's China. In September 1984, British Prime Minister, Margaret Thatcher, signed an agreement in Peking on the future of the colony. China would recover its rights, while committing itself to respecting the present social and economic system in Hong Kong.

The Peking Declaration, as it was styled, only indirectly concerns us here. It is important to point out, however, that the solemn agreement is of value only to the extent that the society of People's China may transform itself accordingly. The chances of a true and loyal cohabitation between the billion 'communised' Chinese and the five or six million capitalist (meaning free) Chinese of Hong Kong will be somewhat precarious if the political regime in Peking does not evolve; to be more precise, Hong Kong's free society will be at risk if China does not *abandon communism*.

The most important of the 'economic zones' created under Deng Xiaoping's direction is named Shenzhen and was set up close to Hong Kong. It came complete with skyscrapers and capitalist banks to handle foreign investments. The symbolic value of Shenzhen is considerable. But it may well be asked whether the economic zones are going to last, surviving Deng the reformer.

In this context, one is bound to note that the enormous Chinese Communist Party with its 40 million members is still very much in charge. A gigantic purge launched in October 1983 was designed to get rid of the 'factionalists' of the Lin Biao tendency, and of the Gang of Four (Mao's widow Jiang Qing and her associates).

Although himself, at 81, a very senior communist citizen, Deng decided in the late summer of 1985 on a mass rejuvenation of the huge Communist Party. Already he had installed protégés as head of the party (General Secretary Hu Yaobang) and head of government (Prime Minister Zhao Ziyang). On the eve of a special party conference in September of that year, he swept away ten of the 24 Politburo members and 64 of the 340 members of the Central Committee which elects the Politburo. Most of those purged were of Deng's generation or slightly younger men, and men of middle years took their seats.

Not all his colleagues were enthusiastic about what Deng was doing to China's economy, and one of his critics, Chen Yun (described ironically as a 'Marxist conservative'), roundly attacked Deng for his reforms. Marxist principles should still rule, said Chen Yun. Deng, well aware that in ideological terms he was squaring the circle, warned his audience that corruption and the 'pernicious influence' of capitalism threatened China's future. But he made it clear that this was just a bit of lingering liturgy for he went on to call on the nation to complete the economic reforms initiated after Mao's death. Deng at any rate, unlike Gorbachev on the evidence, had grasped the fact that you can't cure socialism with more socialism.

It would be bold to forecast that the Deng experiment will endure, or that the 'road' taken will inevitably lead to capitalism. For there is a paradox in that the experiment was launched by a Communist Party which has never yet shown the slightest inclination to relinquish its monopoly of power and whose political or economic 'line' could change suddenly.

What is certain is that, without admitting it in public, Mao Zedong's old comrade had noticed that the flourishing economies of the Far East were all capitalist—notably that his compatriots in Taiwan, heirs to the experiment in microcosm of the defeated leader in the Chinese Civil War, Chiang Kai-shek, enjoyed much higher living standards than the mainland Chinese.

NORTH KOREA

The same illuminating contrast may be observed between the regimented austerity of communist North Korea and the almost unbelievable prosperity achieved in a remarkably short time with capitalist methods in South Korea. The divided countries, indeed, constitute living proof of the superiority of the market economy and free enterprise over centralised socialist planning. What is true of People's China on the one hand, and Taiwan and Hong Kong on the other, is equally true of the two Koreas and of East and West Germany.

In North Korea, however, the element of communism and of dictatorial irrationality are, if anything, even stronger than in China under Mao, so that precise lessons about *socialism* as such are hard to draw. Under Kim Il Sung, North Korea has had, by general expert consensus, the most tightly regimented society on earth. Again, it has developed, more than any other communist country—the Soviet Union not excepted— a *permanent war economy*. Finally, it shares with Romania under Ceausescu the dubious honour of fostering the most extravagant cult of personality of them all.

These are communist rather than socialist characteristics. A country ruled for more than four decades by a megalomaniac planning a war of revenge is hardly a fair model of socialism. I do want to be fair.

VIETNAM

The case of Vietnam is not much more relevant to this little study. It has not (since the death of the founder of the Democratic Republic, Ho Chi Minh, in 1966) been afflicted by a cult of personality. But it is a country that, except for two years or so after the First Indochina War ended in 1954, has been continuously at war since 1946. And although the Americans withdrew in 1973 and the communists overran the south two years later, Vietnam is *still* at war. Twice since then it has been invaded by neighbouring China. And for the past few years it has itself invaded its smaller neighbour Kampuchea (formerly Cambodia), where fighting continues to this day.

When every allowance is made for these extraneous circumstances, however, enough residue is left to enable one to attribute some at least of Vietnam's economic troubles to socialism and to the kind of problems socialism brings in its train: bad planning, corruption, poor management. To these should now be added *unacceptability*. The northerners have had a prolonged dose of socialism, with the usual repression, and the slaughter of at least 50,000 and possibly 100,000 peasants during the 'land reform programme' in the 1950s. The relatively easygoing southerners had got used to relative prosperity, first under the French and later with the arrival of American forces in large numbers. The victorious northerners brought socialism with them, and the southerners do not like it, and have not had time to lump it or to forget happier times, even when earlier wars were raging.

The International Monetary Fund (IMF), reporting in 1982 on the economic situation in Vietnam, noted that per capita income had fallen

from $241 a year in 1976 to $153 in 1981. In March that year, the
General Secretary of the ruling party, Le Duan, reporting to its 5th Congress, admitted that some of the 'many acute problems' facing the
economy stemmed from 'shortcomings and mistakes' by the party itself
and by State officials. The population was growing faster than output
and there were shortages in food and essential consumer goods, including clothing. 'Large numbers of working people' were not being
employed and many enterprises were operating below capacity. As is so
often the case with socialism, there was little discernible relationship
between planning and achievement. The IMF figures showed that
industry had grown by only 1.9 per cent in 1981—whereas the plan had
called for a 4–5 per cent rise. In agriculture, the plan had decreed a 6–7
per cent rise, but actual growth was only 3.2 per cent.

In French colonial times Vietnam was a major rice-exporting country
within South-East Asia, along with Burma and Thailand. In 1981,
however, despite a record harvest of 15 million tons of food grains
(including 12.5 million tons of rice), the Vietnamese still needed to
import 1.3 million tons. The classic situation of agriculture in
communist/socialist regimes was developing fast. In 1981 food production fell by 230,000 tons in South Vietnam—mainly because incentives were poor and southern peasants had started growing only what
they themselves needed. The regime was planning to collectivise most
of the south by 1985, yet by mid-1982 less than 12 per cent of arable
land was worked by the collectives.

Of all communist countries, Vietnam's leaders had had the longest
period at the helm. Le Duan died in 1986. A few months later—in
December—the 'Big Three' of Vietnam, General Secretary Truong
Chinh, ideologue Le Duc Tho and Premier Pham Van Dong, all stepped
down simultaneously. They were 79, 76 and 80, respectively. But
socialism went on.

As one of the 'poor relations' of the communist world Vietnam was
exporting much of its labour to the Soviet bloc. Probably up to half a
million Vietnamese were working in the USSR, Czechoslovakia,
Bulgaria and the German Democratic Republic (East Germany). Many
of them appear to have been drafted for work on the Siberian pipeline to
Western Europe—exchanging the humid heat of South Vietnam for the
permafrost of the Soviet tundra. Hundreds of thousands more had taken
to sea in rickety boats to seek economic or political refuge in the West,
many of them dying before having reached their objectives.

CASTRO'S TROPICAL PARADISE

Along with socialism Cuba offers to its people a flourishing cult of the outsize personality of its *Lider máximo*, Fidel Castro, and wars of foreign conquest as surrogate forces for the Soviet Union, mainly in Africa. It is also a major instigator and participant in political insurgencies in the Caribbean and elsewhere in Latin America.

Surrogate wars are as costly as other kinds but on this score Castro has little to worry him: the bills are picked up by his Soviet protectors. In the 1980s, the best Western estimates were that Cuba was costing the USSR about $1 million a day—roughly the same as that other remote-control satellite in Vietnam. Again, however, our concern here is not with the communist aspects of the regime, but with the performance of centralised socialist planning. Let the Cuban leaders themselves do the talking.

Fidel Castro seized power by force of arms in January 1959, having driven the dictator Fulgencio Batista into exile. Slightly more than twenty years later, in an extraordinary speech before the Cuban National Assembly on 27 December 1979, he reported candidly on the state of the economy after two decades of socialism. Usually Castro—who is prone to make speeches of inordinate length—seeks the maximum publicity for whatever he says. In this case, however, he imposed an unprecedented ban on any reporting of it in the Cuban media. The text nevertheless leaked out, as in 1956 Khrushchev's famous 'secret speech' in Moscow had leaked out. The main points were these: admitting widespread problems, he blamed inefficiency and dishonesty, but also the weather and 'imperialists'. He admitted that Cuba's problems could no longer be blamed on the inexperience of the original revolutionaries.

> During 1979 there were difficulties and shortcomings in connection with imports and from the socialist area . . . by October, only 28 per cent of the 500,000 cubic metres of wood due to be received by us in the year had reached us . . . you can imagine how much this has affected everything, principally buildings, furniture production, the production of packing cases. Wood is not an edible product; it is not eaten. But it affects the economy.
>
> This year, 1979, was one of the worst from the point of view of the fulfilment of deliveries, even affecting the socialist area, in spite of their efforts to comply with delivery.
>
> . . . there are already about 1,200,000 television sets in the country with 200,000 per year now being available. You might say: 'Would it not be better to import more towels and fewer television sets? More sheets and fewer television sets?' . . . that is what we cannot do, because the choice is not available. The friendly countries which supply us with television sets do not have towels or sheets or mattresses to export. On the other hand they have television sets, so we import television sets.

There are no towels because, of a production of 3,600,000, so many are allocated for social expenditure and only so many remain for the population, that one gets a new towel only once every so many years.

If they [the Russians] have forests which they cannot exploit because they do not have the work force, they should make them over to us, even if they are in Siberia; and in Siberia better, because it is not so hot there. And we could send our work brigades to produce wood in Siberia so that we would have all the wood we need at our disposal . . . as our forests do not have wood and Siberia's forests have; if the USSR is our sister—and she is—then those resources are also ours.

We, who have had tens of thousands of workers and international fighters abroad, with 1,200 teachers in Nicaragua, . . . we, who at a given time, have had 36,000 soldiers in Angola, who at another time have had up to 12,000 soldiers in Ethiopia, we who now have builders in Angola, in the Republic of Guinea, in Libya, in Iraq, and who have had them in Vietnam, how are we not going to have 10,000 men if we need them?

Our labour laws today really are protecting the delinquent: in essence our legal system is protecting the delinquent, the vagabond and the absentee; it is not protecting the good worker, who suffers in all this.

Anyone who sees an illegal electric line must report it even though it be his first cousin, even though it be his brother who has installed a new illegal electric line; report it and cut it. It is also the task of judges and public prosecutors, and I say to them, 'You are imposing fines that are too light, and that cannot be.'

Castro added that the whole system must be tightened up and revolutionary fervour revived against ideological enemies.

A year later, in December 1980, Fidel Castro made three major speeches. He was mainly concerned with the possibility of an invasion from the United States, President Reagan having just been elected. The invasion did not, of course, materialise, but all three of Castro's December speeches were permeated with excuses for failures, promises of improvement and exhortations to improve quality and quantity. He dwelt on the impending shortfall in the sugar crop, damage to the tobacco crop, African swine fever and the need for energy conservation. He gave a thinly veiled picture of poverty and undernourishment with distribution difficulties of coffee, rice and cornmeal. The pace of industrialisation, he said, was too slow; labour discipline needed to be strengthened, as did job incentives. Transport was inadequate, with too few taxis and chaotic bus services. A date celebrated with special fervour each year in Cuba is 26 July. That day in 1953 Castro had made a first but abortive attempt to overthrow Batista. On 26 July 1982 he made his usual speech, this time to mark the 29th anniversary of the failed attempt. He made as much as he could of ambitious plans to raise the sugar crops from about 8 million tons in 1980 to 10 million tons by

1985, and to boost the production of nickel—another hard currency earner for Cuba—from 42,000 tons to 100,000 tons annually by late 1984. That was the *good* news—all in the future. The bad news concerned the present and recent past. He revealed that Cuba's debt to the West stood at about $3.5 billion, while there was an overall trade deficit of $1.4 billion, more than half of it with the USSR. He foresaw the abandonment of some projects, short-time working in some industries and virtually no economic growth. Not entirely unfairly, he blamed the country's problems on the low world price for sugar (80 per cent of Cuba's export earnings) and the cost of servicing debts to the West.

Two years earlier, in 1980, Castro's government had carried out a special survey of economic performance. It had found that 90 per cent of manufactured goods did not measure up to quality control standards. Some 41 per cent of managers in the sugar industry were untrained. Vehicle maintenance was poor and there was a chronic lack of spare parts. In ten years living standards had hardly progressed at all.

In several speeches in 1985 Castro took up his schemes of earlier years. Despite a very high growth rate (7.4 per cent) in 1984 he foresaw that his regime's policy of austerity would continue for at least 15 years. On 28 December 1984, he had put it quite frankly: 'We are going to have to put on one side some of our desires and aspirations, but we are going to multiply our capacity for achievement in the future.'

In Cuba as elsewhere, socialism was for the future, and it was a socialist who said so.

9

Third World Socialism

Overwhelmingly, the leaders of the 'emerging' countries opted for socialism when they had won independence or had it conferred upon them by departing colonial powers. Invariably, the option has proved disastrous. Yet the reasons for the choice are easy to understand: they were political and psychological—never economic.

During the struggle for independence the new leaders found a sympathetic hearing for their claims and aspirations among Western communists and socialists. The communists were, of course, interested parties, hoping to set the free colonies of the West on the communist path and bring them into the Soviet orbit. The socialists were more disinterested, in the true sense, but naturally inculcated their ideology into the gratefully receptive minds of their colonial protégés.

As for the said protégés, once they came to power or were in sight of it, the option of socialism became a hard-headed calculation. A centralised economy and a growing bureaucracy became natural devices to perpetuate their hold on power. The economics of capitalism and of the market-place would have deprived them of control over large and probably growing sectors of the population. Thus gratitude, intellectual laziness and cynical expediency combined to foster the installation of socialism.

There was another factor. Capitalism was identified with imperialism in the minds of the new leaders, heavily influenced by Lenin's historically absurd analysis of imperialism as the final phase of capitalism (there were empires before capitalism existed; and the largest surviving empire, in the 1980s, is that of the communist-socialist Soviet Union). The adoption of socialism thus became a moral, or at any rate a political, necessity.

There are so many examples. India's Jawaharlal Nehru was naturally in tune with the rather vague socialism of Kingsley Martin, for so many

100

years identified with the Hampstead leftism of his *New Statesman*. Indonesia's Sukarno thought of himself as a socialist although his interest in economics was minimal. At all events, the *idea* of socialism was compatible with his notions of financial profligacy and the cult of his own personality. The same was true of Kwame Nkrumah of Ghana.

Under its original post-independence leader, U Nu, Burma had turned toward socialism. Unfortunately, General Ne Win, the man who ousted him in 1958, then again in 1962 (having briefly returned power to the civilian politicians), travelled in the same sterile direction. Julius Nyerere of Tanzania tried his own version of socialism which he called *ujamaa* ('familyhood'). It was perhaps even more disastrous than others mentioned.

In French-speaking Africa too, a number of the new leaders opted for socialism. One was Sékou Touré of Guinea. Another was Modibo Keita of Mali. Even Léopold Senghor of Senegal, poet and erudite grammarian (who polished the draft of France's Constitution for the Fourth Republic), declared his country to be on the socialist path. He defined socialism, with closer regard for political sentiment than for the truth, as 'the rational organisation of human society according to the most scientific, the most modern and the most efficient methods'. Fortunately he was less doctrinaire in practice than verbally.

It has to be noted that, by African standards, capitalist Kenya is incomparably more prosperous than socialist Tanzania or Zambia. In French-speaking Africa, the prosperity of the free-enterprise Ivory Coast, under the leadership of Félix Houphouët-Boigny, stands in glaring contrast to its poverty-stricken socialist neighbours. Similarly in Asia, the high living standards of the island republic of Singapore, which has no resources other than its skills and harbour facilities, stands out against the grey drabness of the socialist countries, including Burma. If Taiwan and the giant economy of Japan are introduced into the comparison the failures of socialism, for instance in India, are dazzlingly clear.

INDIA

Nehru and his associates were perhaps social democrats rather than socialists (whereas his daughter, Indira Gandhi, and deferred successor as India's Prime Minister, was a socialist rather than a social democrat, and correspondingly more authoritarian). This meant that his attachment to parliamentary democracy was genuine; which in turn meant that his government's doses of socialism always stopped short of being lethal.

In my book on independence (*The Morning After*, 1963), I made a comparative study of Chinese and Indian socialist planning. In the grip of Mao Zedong's form of totalism, the Chinese People's Republic rushed headlong into the great social and economic disaster of the Great Leap Forward (described earlier). Nehru's attachment to democracy, and a character that fell well short of Mao's ruthlessness, protected India from the worst consequences of unbridled socialism.

In 1951, three years after independence, Nehru launched India's first five-year plan. The goals were fairly modest and luck came in the shape of favourable monsoons and excellent harvests in 1953–4 and 1954–5. Irrigation made great strides and the so-called Community Development Programme seemed to be working toward its goal of making India self-sufficient in food. Real national income rose by more than 18 per cent, and real per capita income by nearly 11 per cent. The rate of investment was 'normal' for hitherto static economies of the Indian kind: it rose during the first five-year plan (1951–6) from 4 per cent of the national income to more than 7 per cent.

The second plan (1956–61) was far more ambitious, and far more socialist, than the first. The lion's share of new investment was earmarked for the public sector: £2,850 million, compared to £1,800 million for the private sector. Admittedly there was a case for heavy investment in the public sector, for apart from the railways—one of the great legacies of the British Raj—India was woefully short of infrastructure—of roads, power stations, schools and training schools.

There, as at all stages of India's history, before and after independence, the great, uncontainable problem was the soaring population. Between 1956 and 1961, the planners had calculated that some 10 million new workers would be looking for jobs. And they knew that it was far beyond the capacity of India's primitive agriculture to absorb them. Industrialisation seemed the answer; although it was of course typical of socialist planning that it was assumed that private enterprise and the law of supply and demand were too 'risky' to be trusted to fill the need.

In the event, private enterprise, though relatively starved of funds by the planners, did spectacularly better than public. In the ten years of the first two plans, the output of the private enterprises had soared by anything between 350 per cent and 1,000 per cent. India had become an important manufacturing nation producing a range of goods from bicycles to diesel-electric motors, from sewing machines to refrigerators, both for the home market and for export. Overall, industrial output had risen between 110 per cent and 120 per cent. Great strides had been made in communications and electrification, in irrigation and fertilisers, in oil and machine tools. The shortcomings, however, typified the irresponsible optimism of bureaucrats planning a country's economic development from the centre. There were, for instance, perilously optimistic assumptions about where the money was to come from to meet the bills, and other errors. There were in fact three major sins of assumption:

(1) that the population would rise by only 1.25 per cent a year. In fact, it rose by 2 per cent. In a population as large as India's already was, this meant an additional 17 million mouths, and it was estimated that India's population had reached 425 million in 1960–61, instead of the assumed 408 million;

(2) that the encouraging food crops of the first plan would continue. In fact, the monsoon failed in 1957. Grain production dropped by 6.7 million tons and food prices soared by 10 per cent in one year. The planners had assumed that India would not need to import more than 6 million tons of food over the five-year period. In reality, the need was of the order of 15 million tons;

(3) that India's foreign exchange requirements ('resources to be raised externally,' as the planners airily expressed it) would be about £600 million (in addition to India's own sterling balances, estimated at £150 million) and would easily be forthcoming. The underlying assumption was that the terms of trade would continue to be as favourable to India as they had been in 1954–5. Disaster: they fell back to the 1952–4 level. The trade gap widened alarmingly from £47 million—relatively manageable—to £218 million.

In one respect, however, India was lucky. The Indians it turned out, had friends—good, generous *capitalist* friends—ready to rescue Nehru from the consequences of his planners' assumptions. The Eisenhower administration decided to meet India's food import gap from American agricultural surpluses, under the famous Public Law 480, and there would be no charge. In 1958 Britain, West Germany and Japan joined with the USA to form the 'aid India club'.

It is perhaps worth quoting the rather grandiose eight basic decisions that were to govern Nehru's and his planners' 'grand strategy in the war against poverty' (as the second five-year plan was termed), in that they typify the woolly thinking inseparable from social democracy:

(1) the second plan must be big—big enough and powerful enough to begin to lift the Indian economy across the 'threshold' to a developed nation;

(2) India will develop first and above all its agriculture and its rural people;

(3) India will develop its industries—but with a careful balancing of large and small industry, of the heavy industries basic to economic growth, and the traditional small and hand industries essential to employment and social stability;

(4) India will increase living standards and consumption at the same time that it builds its industries;

(5) India will take advantage of every possible way of growth consistent with democracy to develop the nation and its people;

(6) India will seek the development of all groups and classes among its people, and of all regions of the nation, so that there may be a growing equality of income and opportunity;

(7) India will at every step of its progress associate the people in the villages and districts with planning and development, so that their initiative, energies and co-operation are awakened and assured, and may serve as the constructive and creative instrument of development itself;

(8) India will, in all its plans and policies, set as its highest single purpose the development of the individual and his advancement in human freedom.

The second point was merely pious. If it meant anything it implied that agriculture had a high investment priority. In fact, the second plan allotted only 11 per cent of the budget to agriculture, compared to 50 per cent for industry (the basic Stalinist error from which the socialist regimes of Eastern Europe, including Russia, all suffer). Under the third plan, agriculture was to get 14 per cent—better, but still inadequate, given the size of the problem.

The sixth decision also contained its element of self-righteous piety. The development of 'all groups and classes' sounded admirably egalitarian, and was indeed in line with Nehru's constitution which forbade discrimination against the *harijans* or 'untouchables'. That this was a provision on paper only could be observed by anybody dropping in at random on any of India's 600,000 villages. Some 80 million Indians remained condemned to clean the latrines and sweep the streets, no matter what the constitution or the sixth basic decision might say. Similarly, another legacy of Hinduism—the sacred cow—made a nonsense of planning assumptions. Diseased but sacrosanct, some 250 million holy cows competed with the people for India's scarce food resources.

The most important aspect of the basic assumptions, however, was the pursuit of incompatible objectives: centralised planning *and* individual freedom; tolerance of private enterprise *and* priority of investment for the State; creation of large-scale industries *and* stimulation and protection of the economically unproductive cottage crafts, dear to the heart of Mahatma Gandhi.

Given the performance of private industry in the face of governmental obstacles, including excessively high taxes, there is little doubt that it could, under more favourable conditions, have gone a long way toward solving India's perennial problem of poverty. But that would not have suited the planners. From the start Nehru had vested the Planning Commission with virtually limitless economic powers, under the Prime Minister's own chairmanship. Starting from preconceived socialist theory, instead of adapting the economic lessons of history to India's special problems, India's planners made the usual mistakes of *dirigiste* planning. In economic terms their fundamental error was to give priority to industry over agriculture. In political and philosophical terms they overlooked the clear correlation between economic and political freedom. True centralised planning can be followed through in practice only when the State conscripts and directs labour, requisitions all materials and smashes any opposition that is bound to manifest itself. Fortunately, India was saved by its attachment to democracy, not its belief in socialism. Something had to give and (under Nehru, at least) it was usually socialism.

Another thing saved India from the worst the planners could inflict: the capitalist friends I mentioned earlier. In his interesting study, *Leaders* (1982), Richard Nixon wrote:

> India found productivity from the bottom up. Instead on the economic front, it got ideology from the top down, with layer upon layer of flypaper bureaucracy to snare the feet of anything that moved. The United States alone provided India with more than $9 billion of aid since independence. But this has gone to remedy the results of socialist failure rather than to build the foundations of a self-sustaining economy. [p. 273]

It is important to add that over the past few years, India has made quite remarkable economic progress—by liberalising an excessively socialised economy. Robert McNamara, former President of the World Bank, made a brief survey of India's progress in the *International Herald Tribune* (13 June 1985): 'In 1965, following the advice of international agronomists, especially Americans, the Indian authorities introduced new varieties of grain, including rice. This experiment was dubbed the Green Revolution. It proved a spectacular success. Despite two periods of drought (1979–80 and 1982), which not long before would have caused famine, the production of foodstuffs has gone on increasing.'

In 1965, the base year, India produced only 81 million tons of grain; in 1984 India's farmers, scattered in their 600,000 villages, beat all records with a total production of 153 million tons, a rise of 72 million tons. Nowadays India manages to feed itself, without needing either costly imports of foodstuffs or excessive international aid programmes (which in fact account for only 7 per cent of the development budget).

India is no longer a beggar country. It has undergone an astonishing transformation.

In contrast with so many countries of the Third World, India is not a debtor—another remarkable achievement. A considerable growth in domestic sources of energy reduced imports of petroleum products from 63 per cent of consumption in 1979 to only 37 per cent in 1983. Moreover, thanks to heavy investment, largely based on private savings, India has achieved an annual economic growth rate of 5.1 per cent. And all this despite the fact that, with an average yearly income of only $260, India is still one of the poorest countries in the world.

India's achievement is important, but so too are the reasons for it. Robert McNamara attributes the growth in India's food production (apart from the Green Revolution) to a policy of liberalising farm prices. As a result productivity grew fast, as did total production. The same applies to other sectors of the economy. By reducing tariffs on imports Indira Gandhi's government made local industry more competitive and greatly stimulated the private sector. India's exports grew accordingly.

It is true that central planning continues under Mrs Gandhi's son, Rajiv, but it is now linked to an economy that is far more liberal than it had been in the early years of independence, and therefore does much less harm. Thus India, which was dying of hunger during its socialist period, is now self-sufficient to the extent that it has abandoned the cause of ailment.

BURMA

By common consent the Burmese are by nature easygoing and charming. Yet xenophobia is an important element in Burma's history and national character. It is Burma's misfortune that its dictator since 1962 (without counting his previous short-lived rule in 1958), General Ne Win, chose to inflict both a Marxist socialist experiment and official xenophobia upon the many peoples of Burma. It took Ne Win about 12 years to complete the ruination of Burma which had begun under the inefficient civilian politicians whom he displaced.

In January 1948 Burma became the first of Britain's imperial possessions to gain its independence. With its enormous mineral resources, its rice and its timber, it had every right to expect a flourishing economic future. In their innocence U Nu and his colleagues told their people that before very long each family could expect a house and a car of their own and no less than £1,500 a year. Alas by 1974, the average family income at only £200 a year was one of the world's lowest. Burma had absorbed some hundreds of millions of dollars in foreign aid with nothing to show for it, and instead of exporting 3 million tons of rice, as it did in the bad old colonial days, the silos were empty and food riots not uncommon. Burma's civilian politicians had at least the attraction of inefficiency and an easygoing Buddhist approach to government. Ne Win, half-Chinese and energetic, set Burma on the road to poverty with military efficiency. 'Shared scarcity' was Hugh Tinker's kind euphemism for it. I prefer to call it the 'cult of scarcity'.

Ne Win set out his ideas in a manifesto, *The Burmese Way to Socialism*, which proclaimed two mutually antithetical principles: a commitment to Marxism and the promise of 'a new society for all, economically secure and morally better'. It was the commitment to Marxism that won.

More than 90 per cent of Burma's commerce and industry was nationalised, creating drastic shortages of all commodities on the home market and—the natural consequence—widespread corruption and a flourishing black market, despite severe penalties. In agriculture Ne Win went even further than his distant mentors of the Soviet Union, for instance, by 'nationalising' onions, potatoes and beans. All three items promptly disappeared since the farmers now saw no special reason to produce them. Ne Win's response was typically authoritarian. He decontrolled onions, potatoes and beans; all three rapidly reappeared on the market. He then pounced on the private traders who were handling the reborn items, ordering the army to seize the more successful firms and jailing the successful owners.

As for the xenophobia, Ne Win simply stopped issuing import licences to foreign firms trading in Burma and denied them access to foreign currency. The foreigners had a simple choice: be nationalised or go bust. Most of them left Burma. Tourism was banned and so were foreign journalists. In its xenophobic vacuum Burma speeded up its socialist journey into abject poverty.

TANZANIA

Julius Nyerere, president of Tanzania (a neologistic amalgam of Tanganyika and Zanzibar) from 1961 to 1985, must be granted a natural talent for public relations. A mild-mannered little man with a soft voice, he rapidly built up a reputation for moderation in Westminster, Whitehall, and Fleet Street. In fact he has shown himself one of the most extreme of the post-independence leaders of Black Africa. The myth, however, prevails. It is distinctly bad form to hint that perhaps, after all, Nyerere is not a 'moderate'.

On a State visit to Britain in 1975 the moderate Mr Nyerere had this to say: 'In one world, as in one State, when I am rich because you are poor, and I am poor because you are rich, the transfer of wealth from rich to poor is a matter of right: it is not an appropriate matter of charity.'

This curious philosophy, which incidentally is economic nonsense, gained astonishingly wide acceptance. For instance it underlies one of the more absurd documents of recent times, the Brandt Report of 1981, in the compilation of which a former British Prime Minister, Edward Heath, played a leading part. The Brandt Report might indeed have been written as a personal favour to Julius Nyerere, and advocated a massive transfer of wealth from the 'rich North' to the 'poor South', of which it could be said, on the basis of simple observation, that it would be a recipe for the rapid further enrichment of an already corrupt official class in the 'developing' countries with no effect upon the living standards of Third World populations.

I am, however, digressing. The myths of development aid programme and of Nyerere's alleged moderation were brilliantly exploded in an article by Peter Bauer and John O'Sullivan in the *Spectator*, 25 June 1977. By then the irreparable damage inflicted on his country by President Nyerere was an accomplished fact. From it I quote:

> Some regimes do not stop at persecuting minorities. Dr Nyerere's government in Tanzania has in the last decade forcibly moved millions of people into collectivised villages and sometimes simply into the bush. Among the methods of encouragement employed are the destruction of existing homes, physical force, and barring recalcitrant elements from such social facilities as communal transport, beer shops, ceremonial dances and cattle auctions. The numbers of people subjected to this new life certainly run into millions. Some estimates are as high as six to eight million (*Washington Post*, 6 May 1975) and even 13 million (*The Times*, 20 April 1977) out of a total population of 15 million.

The examples of Burma and Tanzania are admittedly more extreme than those of other socialist experiments, outside the communist countries. But the fact that they are more extreme than some merely proves the points made throughout this book. The more extreme the socialism, the more extreme the impoverishment. And the more extreme the socialism, the greater the coercion and sufferings of the population. The contradiction between socialism and liberty is total: the more socialism, the less liberty. The social democrat who, in the last resort, stops short of full socialism because he values democracy understands these points instinctively, although he is not necessarily willing to concede them intellectually.

10

Welfare Socialism

George Bernard Shaw, in the *Intelligent Woman's Guides* in the 1920s
and 1930s, used to delight in reminding his (presumably feminine)
audience that all countries, including capitalist ones, practised
communism in some aspects of daily life. His examples included roads,
railways and postal services. Similarly one might truly say that all
countries, including 'capitalist' ones, practise socialism to some degree
or other.

Some degree of socialism may indeed be necessary. The trouble is to
establish how much is needed and where to draw the line. For my part, I
favour socialist welfare—for those who need it. The trouble with welfare
socialism as introduced into Britain in the post-war Labour government
of Clement Attlee is that it is indiscriminate, so that even people who do
not need it receive it. I shall have more to say on the British example,
and there is no shortage of others in the Western world. I shall also, in
this chapter, take a selective look at France, Sweden, West Germany,
Austria and the great United States of America—with a passing glance
at Australia.

FRANCE—AND BRITAIN

The example of France is particularly apposite, for the performance in
office of the Socialist Communist government which governed the
French Republic in the first phase of President François Mitterrand's
septennat was there for all to see. When Mitterrand's coalition came to
power in May 1981 France had had about two decades of unprecedented
economic growth, rising standards of living and general prosperity. In
less than two years socialism had, in effect, ruined the country. It was an
amazing, if negative, achievement.

In 1955 a Swiss journalist called Herbert Luthy wrote a book that

109

caused a sensation in France. Its title, in French, was *La France a l'heure de son clocher* (the English translation of which was *France Keeps Its Own Time*). The France Luthy was writing about was backward in comparison with its neighbours and rivals. Capital equipment was obsolete; investment was inadequate. Any economist bold enough to extrapolate from the data given by Luthy would have concluded that France in two or three decades would find itself, let us say, the 'Albania' of Western Europe. Instead, the opposite happened. General Charles de Gaulle came to power in 1958, and gave priority to bringing the expensive Algerian war to a close. He brought in the experienced former Prime Minister, Antoine Pinay, as Finance Minister, and Pinay dealt with French inflation by the simple expedient of knocking off the last two noughts of France's currency and creating a 'heavy franc'. Recovery and expansion really got under way in 1962. Over the next ten years (1962–72) France's gross national product (GNP) grew from $52,583 million to $273,806 million. In comparison the British economy, which suffered from creeping socialism, grew from an initially favourable GNP of $62,668 million to no more than $188,543 million. During the whole of the period between 1962 and 1981 France enjoyed the blessings of relative stability under de Gaulle's Fifth Republic, under a Constitution tailor-made for de Gaulle. But the real point was that during this entire period, although France itself had a welfare socialism of its own, the country's finances were under the direction of able conservative technicians, including Valéry Giscard d'Estaing, later to become President of the Republic before his defeat at the hands of François Mitterrand. In other words, France had been doing pretty well with *minimal* socialism.

I must be fair to the French Socialists (although fairness is hardly due to the Moscow-line Stalinist French Communist Party which Mitterrand had taken into the coalition because he thought it would be safer to have Communists inside than outside his government). The coalition took over at a time of deepening international recession. In France itself unemployment had been mounting, and was past the two million mark. French socialist doctrine (as is true of socialism everywhere) had an easy prescription for this kind of situation: spend, spend, spend! And nationalise, nationalise, nationalise! So the government nationalised nearly all the banks and insurance companies and created some 200,000 phony jobs in the public sector. Soon, government spending rose uncontrollably. So did unemployment; as did inflation, which was soon double the British rate, and four times the German.

In the non-communist world there are two standard short-term remedies for this kind of situation: borrow or print money. The French government did both. It borrowed wildly abroad and kept the printing presses busy. Faced with rising costs and increasing labour militancy, private industry found itself becoming rapidly uncompetitive in the world's markets—exactly as Britain's had during the long years of creeping socialism. The only difference was that the French were moving downhill faster than the British did. Twice the government devalued the franc. Even that was not enough. The grand climax came in March 1983 with a *third* devaluation and a budget of savage austerity.

The Finance Minister, Jacques Delors, having presided over this man-made ruination, now forced the French taxpayers to pay the price for official follies. For the record the government introduced a temporary but compulsory savings plan, equivalent to 10 per cent of income tax, and a new tax on wealth, from which only the truly poor were to be exempt. In addition a surcharge equivalent to 1 per cent of income tax was imposed. All this would yield about 11 billion francs, which would be used to balance, more or less, the social security fund.

But of all the measures published at that time, the most unpopular was undoubtedly the annual limit of 2,000 francs per adult for those who would feel the curious need to take their holidays abroad. For children the limit was fixed at 1,000 francs each. Henceforth French families were forbidden to use their credit cards outside metropolitan France.

To be fair one should add that some of the measures taken at that time of panic—notably the restrictions in foreign currency allocations to French tourists and the exceptional increase of 1 per cent on income tax—were later cancelled. In fact such measures are hardly open to criticism, given the emergency faced by the government. Any other governmental team would have acted in the same way, faced with an acute crisis characterised by a frightening rise in the rate of inflation and a no less frightening dwindling of hard currency reserves. That was not the real issue, however. The essential point was that this crisis in particular had been created from start to finish by the systematic and precipitate application of *socialist* measures because they happened to have been stated in the programme of the parties of the Left now in power.

Let us continue with our balance sheet. Starting on 1 April 1983 all charges for public utilities, including gas, electricity, the telephone service and the railways, were raised by 8 per cent. Previously anticipated spending was to be reduced by 15 billion francs, while revenues were to be increased by means of a special tax on gasoline products. Already the deficit on external trade had reached around 100 billion francs. The new measures, however were supposed to reduce internal consumption by about 65 billion francs at the end of 1983—that is, by the equivalent of 2 per cent of GNP.

Two years later, the French voters were still assessing the damage of that first wave of socialising folly, scarcely mitigated by the policy of austerity. In March 1985, in tens of thousands, farm workers left their farms to take to the streets. Monster demonstrations were staged to protest against falling incomes. Again let us be fair: in this lamentable situation, the Socialist government (from which by now the Communist Party had departed) was only partly to blame. The European Community, with its mountain of butter, its milk river and its wine lake, had its share of responsibility. But the Socialists could hardly boast that their agricultural policy had been a success.

In any case, this was not all. The Communist-controlled trade union confederation, the CGT, launched large-scale strikes. The exchange deficit reached 6.5 billion francs. In contrast to President Reagan's capitalist America, socialist France seemed unable to create new jobs. (In the United Kingdom over several years, Prime Minister Thatcher's 'monetarist' policy had only partially lived up to expectations, probably because of the length and scope of the socialist experiment, even in periods of Conservative rule. But the policy of encouraging small enterprises was beginning to bring results in 1985 with the creation of some 600,000 jobs. This, however, was not enough to compensate for the job losses in such old industries as coal and steel.)

Between 1974 and May 1981 the number of jobs in France had increased by several hundred thousand, but between 1981 and 1985 there had been a job loss of 500,000.

At the end of March 1985 Edith Cresson, Minister for Industrial Redeployment and External Trade, drew up an impressive balance sheet for the nationalised industries. She noted a 'spectacular financial recovery on the part of the six groups nationalised in 1982', whose consolidated net profits in 1984 had reached around 3 billion francs (according to her figures), as compared with a loss of 1.4 billion francs in 1981. On analysis it appeared that this encouraging view applied in fact and specifically only to Péchiney, Saint-Gobain, CGE, Thomson, Rhône-Poulenc, and Bull. But Mme Cresson had remained silent on the much less satisfactory balance sheet of other nationalised industries: including the State-owned Renault (which was 12 billion francs in the red in 1984), CDF-Chimie (whose losses reached about 800 million francs), Sacilor, and Usinor. The steel industry had losses of 8 billion francs during that period.

This brought an apposite comment from a journalist commentator, Elizabeth Chavelet: 'This year still, the 13.6 billion in capital grants to the nationalised industries will be "eaten up" by the enterprises that are not doing very well. Renault and the steel industry will get the lion's share' (*Figaro*, 28 March 1985).

A few days later the French employers' federation, the CNPF, complained that the competitiveness of French enterprises was still inadequate, as witnessed by the fact that, over the past five years, France's share in world trade had diminished.

In France as in Britain and elsewhere, it is always the taxpayers (that is, the people) who meet the bills when nationalised industries are doing badly. Let us cheer the successes. But in the long term, every industry in each industrialised country has to face the competition of the international market. When competitiveness is diminishing the burden becomes heavier. The British have been through it all; now it is the turn of the French.

It has to be said that it is still too early to draw up a valid balance sheet for the socialist experiment in France. Perspective is lacking. It will be up to the free-enterprise parties, the RPR-UDF, who defeated the socialists in the elections of 1986—and one of whose leaders, Jacques Chirac, became the new Prime Minister—to discover for themselves how long-lasting the effects will be. The damage done is there, visible and palpable. On the whole the French voters appear to be aware of it, on the evidence of the public opinion polls. What cannot yet be said is whether the situation is reversible, and how long it will take to undo the harm done. In France, as already in Britain, privatisation will succeed nationalisation. On the early evidence this experiment appears to be highly successful in Britain, but it is still too early to affirm that the same will be true of France.

Once again, a comparison between these two countries, both brothers and rivals, is instructive. By a big majority the British demonstrated, in the aftermath of World War Two, that they *wanted* socialism, in which they saw a long-term solution of the ills of capitalism—insecurity, cyclical crises, economic depression, unemployment and general misery. Starting from the absolute zero of an economy ruined by the war, the Labour Party in six years laid the bases of a system that was supposed to ensure full employment and universal social security. The British people discovered, very late, that nationalised industries and social charges, along with the rest of the socialist baggage, constituted a gua antee of long-term economic decline, through inflation and reduced c mpetitiveness in international markets. Moreover, it did not even guarantee full employment.

In comparison France in 1981 had no real *need* o socialism. The Socialists and their temporary allies the Communists ame to power at the tail end of a period of spectacular expansion duri g which France, which at the outset had been relatively backward, ove rtook Britain with an astonishing speed. Not only had France no need o socialism, but the French, by a sizeable majority, did not even *wan* it. The Socialist-

Communist alliance of François Mitterrand did not 'win' the elections of 1981. A divided Right lost them, partly because of its divisions, but partly also because the French electorate had no desire to leave Valéry Giscard d'Estaing in charge of the Elysée Palace for a further period of seven years.

Such observations do not alter reality in any way. Once in power the Socialists and Communists lost no time in carrying out what they had promised, or threatened, to do—to nationalise and to raise public expenditure. As the French commentator Jean-Claude Casanova correctly reminded Premier Laurent Fabius, when the latter was merely the minister in charge of budgetary drafting, he had declared in October 1981: 'Employment starts with expansion' and 'expansion starts with increased public expenditure.' (See the Paris news magazine, *L'Express*, of 27 September 1985.)

The prescribed dose of socialism, both dogmatic and unnecessary, swiftly brought the results felt by the French people. Alarmed by the results, the government launched a policy of austerity—the classical remedy. At least may it be said that in a democratic country such as France, it would be possible for the people to cure the nation of its dose of socialism by changing direction; whereas in the USSR, where the source of the damage is permanently installed, Mikhail Gorbachev cannot abandon the doctrine which alone justifies the Party's monopoly of power.

The austerity campaign responded to the public mood in the sense that it took account of public alarm at the (predictable) outcome of Mitterrand's initial socialist policies. In March 1986 the public mood was given its chance to express itself and brought to office a centre-right coalition headed by the new Prime Minister, Jacques Chirac. Amidst fierce controversy, an oddity of General de Gaulle's Constitution of the Fifth Republic now came into play. The General wanted a minimum of seven years in supreme office so the Constitution laid down that the President should have a guaranteed *septennat* in the Elysée Palace. The National Assembly, however, was elected for only four years.

In opposition Mitterrand had been scornfully critical of the Gaullian Constitution. Now he saw the advantage of it. Although many public figures—especially President Giscard's ex-Prime Minister Raymond Barre—thought it outrageous that Mitterrand should not present himself for re-election (or rejection) at the pools, he was strictly within his rights in staying where he was, even though the incoming government was proposing to undo his work. His power as President, though not absolute, was far from negligible. On 26 March, a few days after Chirac had formed his first government, President Mitterrand announced that he would veto decrees designed to undo the past government's achievements on social reform. On 9 April, he spelled it out to the Cabinet (over which he presided as of right): he would not sign decrees for the privatisation of State sectors nationalised before 1981. This fore-shadowed a protracted period of President-versus-Prime Minister infighting in Parliament.

Thus began France's unprecedented experiment of 'cohabitation' between a socialist President and an anti-socialist Premier. In the face of this obstacle Chirac launched an optimistic economic strategy of shifting to a freer market economy including the privatisation of major banking, financial and industrial State holdings. It was too early, when these lines were written in late 1986, to judge the outcome of the con-stitutional power struggle.

THE BRITISH SICKNESS

To say that Britain's economic and social problems had been partly caused, and certainly aggravated, by the two long post-Attlee periods of Labour rule (1964–70 and 1974–79) would be true, but only part of the truth. The deeper problem, scarcely perceived by the bulk of traditional Labour voters, was that the Labour Party had been progressively pene-trated and increasingly taken over by the totalist Left, committed to 'irreversible' socialism.

As I have said the Attlee–Bevin government of the immediate post-war years, though committed to welfare and State sector socialism, was undoubtedly anti-communist and indeed anti-totalist in a broader sense. In 1966 the Harold Wilson government was at least ready to recognise the problem officially. When the country was almost paralysed by a pro-longed seamen's strike, Mr Wilson, in a speech on 28 June, told the House of Commons:

> The House will be aware that the Communist Party, unlike the major politi-cal parties, has at its disposal an efficient and disciplined industrial apparatus controlled from Communist Party headquarters. No major strike occurs anywhere in this country in any sector of industry in which that apparatus fails to concern itself.

During his second administration, in contrast, Mr Wilson never once publicly mentioned the communist or Marxist threat to his own party. In 1973, Labour, skilfully manipulated by the extremists, had discon-tinued the famous list of 'proscribed organisations'—that is, of a large number of Communist and Trotskyist organisations which Labour Party members were not allowed to join. The floodgates were now open and the extremists rushed in.

By 1978, 17 of the 29 members of the National Executive Committee

(NEC) of the Labour Party were of the extreme Left. More and more constituency organisations were being taken over by Trotskyists of the 'Militant Tendency' (the fancy name of a secret party whose real name was the Revolutionary Socialist League). No wonder the NEC, at the end of 1975, had turned down a report (by Labour's National Agent, Reg—later Lord—Underhill) on the extremist penetration of the party. Increasingly, too, the trade union movement was falling under extremist control, with certain honourable exceptions, notably the Electricians' Union which its energetic, ex-Communist leader Frank (later Lord) Chapple had rescued from a Communist leadership that had been fraudulently elected.[1]

I pause here to deal with a dangerous semantic confusion. There is a long-standing convention in the newspaper and publishing worlds in Britain—carefully fostered, on the basis of flimsy case histories, by Fleet Street's lawyers—that it is libellous to call somebody a 'communist' unless he or she is actually a member of the Communist Party. This suits the communists very well, especially those who are not actually party members. Am I contradicting myself? Not in the least. Some of the most dangerous communists—men like the KGB spies H.A.R. ('Kim') Philby, or Klaus Fuchs—never joined the party.

Many timid souls draw consolation from the fact that much of the penetration of the Labour Party has been the work of so-called 'Trotskyist' groups such as Militant or the Socialist Workers' Party. But to distinguish such groups from the Communist Party is an absurdity, for it amounts to saying that the original Trotsky, one of the leaders of the communist revolution in Russia, was not a communist. The absurdity is compounded by the fact that the Communist Party of Great Britain (CPGB) split in 1984. Dyed-in-the-wool, pro-Moscow hardliners were expelled from the party, though they retained control of the communist daily, *Morning Star*, and formed the New Communist Party. The old CPGB started calling itself 'Eurocommunist', to take its distance from Moscow.

The only sensible course is to use 'communist' and 'communism' as generic terms, much as 'Christian' and 'Christianity' in normal usage. Just as there are many varieties of Christian (such as Roman Catholic, Baptist, Seventh Day Adventist, etc.) so there are many varieties of communists. In the last analysis it will make no noticeable difference which variety or varieties of communist control the Labour Party if it is voted back to office without having purged itself of the totalists in its midst. Absolute socialism will be there to stay. And the enormous subversive apparatus of the Soviet Union would soon bring Britain under Soviet control even if people calling themselves 'Eurocommunists' or 'Trotskyists' controlled a ruling Labour Party.

Not surprisingly, in view of the process I have briefly described, the Labour Party's two Manifestoes of 1974, and its Programme in 1976, were Marxist documents, the latter, in particular, indistinguishable in essentials from the Programme of the CPGB.

On 16 March 1976, Harold Wilson astonished his colleagues and the country by announcing his resignation as party leader and Prime Minister. Under his successor, James Callaghan, the largely extremist leadership of the trades unions further consolidated their grip on the Labour Party. Already an informal arrangement known rather grandly as the 'Social Contract' gave the trades unions a *de facto* 'right' to be consulted by the government on all aspects of economic policy. The Social Contract had been imposed on Labour by the then leader of the giant Transport and General Workers' Union, Jack Jones, an extreme leftist though not formally a member of the Communist Party (though his wife was). As Woodrow Wyatt put it, stating no more than the truth, the Social Contract, as enshrined in the 1976 Programme, was designed to transform Britain before very long into an East European State.[2]

With inflation running at 20–25 per cent (with a 'high' of 27 per cent), the Social Contract dramatically accelerated Britain's industrial decline. The apparently irresistible march of socialism, however, foundered on Mr Callaghan's 'winter of discontent' in late 1978 and early 1979. Bakery workers stopped making bread and provincial journalists stopped making newspapers; lorry drivers stopped driving; train drivers immobilised trains; water and sewerage workers stopped providing their indispensable services. In some places the dead went unburied and patients were turned away from hospitals, while refuse went uncollected.

In February 1979 a lengthy and verbose joint statement by the government and the Trades Union Congress, grandly known as the 'concordat', enshrined the party's capitulation to the extremists. Fortunately the people had had enough. On 3 May they voted the new Conservative leader, Mrs Margaret Thatcher, to power with an absolute parliamentary majority of more than 40 seats, on an explicitly antisocialist programme.

When these lines were written the historical perspective was still too short to pass judgement on the success of 'Thatcherism', but some preliminary observations could be made:

(1) 'Privatisation' was a success. In their millions ordinary people rushed to buy shares in the previously loss-making State concerns, such as British Telecom and British Gas. This was *popular*, as distinct from the phony public ownership of key industries;

(2) The battle against inflation, though not fully won, had certainly brought important results, with a reduction of the annual rate of

increase in prices from around 25 per cent to 2 or 3 per cent. As in the US, lower taxes had increased revenues—a paradox only for socialists who cannot understand that punitive taxes drive tax-payers abroad or underground and discourage enterprise.

(3) On the adverse side the Welfare State went on its merry, bloated way. Despite complaints of declining service, queues and delays for major operations and the closing of public wards, the hard fact was that the cost of the National Health Service rose by 20 per cent in real terms between 1979 and 1986. An additional 69,000 employees had been taken on and the cost continued to rise at 3 per cent a year in real terms. This was one aspect of socialism that seemed in no danger of extinction.

On all sides it seemed to be agreed that unemployment remained unacceptably high. But of course, much hinged on definitions of 'unemployed'. The 'Plowden Report'* in August 1986 had concluded, after meticulous analysis, that no more than 29 per cent of those officially unemployed were genuinely out of work. Thus of the official total of 3.2 million only between 900,000 and 1 million were truly unemployed. Of the total, between 320,000 and 420,000 were probably *unemployable* for health or other reasons, and were caught in the 'poverty trap'. About 32 per cent of the total worked for cash—untaxed—on the 'black economy'.

Overall, Britain's economic situation and prospects were unquestionably far better under an anti-socialist than under a socialist government. In this context what was the Labour Party offering the voting public? First, under the Shadow Chancellor of the Exchequer, Roy Hattersley, a programme of vastly increased public expenditure—by at least £28 billion a year and possibly as much as £35 billion, depending on the calculation. All this, of course, would be financed by vastly increased taxation (which as the Reaganite experience in America has shown would not necessarily increase revenue). The aim was to reduce unemployment rapidly by a million.

And what of privatisation? When the Labour Party held its annual conference at Blackpool in October 1986, extremist demands for wholesale re-nationalisation were rejected. But the conference confirmed that British Telecom and British Gas would be taken back into public ownership. This was a time for euphemisms. 'Nationalisation' was out; instead, the formula was 'social ownership', defined, though with a minimum of precision, as companies owned neither by private capital nor by central government, and responsive to the needs of

---

* The report of a Committee for Research into Public Attitudes by a group of industrialists chaired by Lord Plowden.

workers and customers. To this end, said Mr Hattersley, local authorities would have to be given the finance to invest in and own companies in their own areas. As in other countries the patent failure of socialism was not going to discourage socialist parties.

The biggest sensation of the Labour conference, however, was in defence. The new party leader, Neil Kinnock, committed Britain to a non-nuclear policy and said he would close down the American bases in Britain. He also said that Britain would remain in NATO, with no apparent awareness that he was expressing self-contradictory propositions. Defence is not central to the argument of this book. Mr Kinnock's anti-nuclear and anti-American pledges are relevant, however, in that they powerfully reinforce the view I expressed earlier—that an extremist-dominated Labour government would not only turn Britain into a copy of an East European satellite, but would also, in short order, fall under Soviet domination.*

THE SWEDISH MODEL

Swedish socialism has certain unique features. For one thing, it has been 'going strong' for a long time: Social Democratic governments were in power continuously for 44 years, until the very left-wing Prime Minister, the late Olof Palme, fell in 1976. But the mildly 'conservative' government which took over did virtually nothing to counter the trend. By the Swedish socialism was firmly established by national consensus and by inertia. In 1982 Palme came back to power and the process resumed and continued even after Palme was murdered early in 1986.

The most remarkable aspect of Swedish socialism is that, in contrast to most other kinds (ranging from, say, the USSR to the United Kingdom), nationalisation of private companies was, by and large, avoided. The idea was not that the State should grab the means of pro-

---

* Let us note in passing that an acute case of the socialist disease had overtaken Australia by the summer of 1986. In an article in *The Times* of 19 August, David Butler, Fellow of Nuffield College, Oxford, put it in these words: 'The Australian economy—and with it Australian politics—are in crisis. Today Paul Keating, the Hawke government's tough, pragmatic young Treasurer, will unveil the harshest and least socialist budget ever framed by a Labour government in Australia. Keating wants to slash the government deficit by billions of dollars, hoping that his cuts will be enough to check a run on the Australian currency which, since 1984, has fallen from 92 cents to the US dollar to a mere 60 cents.

'The present trouble echoes Britain's in 1976—a left-of-centre government faced by an amalgam of inflation, high interest rates, a balance of payments deficit and an uncertain deal with the unions. And, as in 1976, the Australians have suddenly realised how bad things are. . . .'

duction; rather, that it should grab the production itself. In other words, the wealth produced by Swedish industry, and the money earned by individuals was in effect confiscated by the State, in return for the most universal welfare schemes on earth.

The Swedes had other things going for them. One was industrial peace on an almost unrivalled scale (with only Switzerland as a competitor). This went back to the famous Saltsjöbaden agreement of 1938, which repudiated strikes without actually outlawing them. The Swedes, too, enjoyed peace in the more normal sense, meaning the absence of war. Previously warlike, they had abandoned war as an instrument of policy starting in 1815, and lived through two world wars without actually getting involved—a sure-fire recipe for prosperity.

For about three decades, Swedish socialism appeared to be a going concern. The Swedes had apparently achieved the impossible: free enterprise and socialism were cohabiting, and Sweden had achieved one of the highest standards of living in the world with the widest distribution of social benefits. Despite high spending on defence (to defend their neutrality), the Swedes always managed, or so it seemed, to keep afloat. To complete the picture, Sweden had high-grade iron ore in abundance; a flourishing paper and pulp industry served by immense forests; and waterpower for the asking. And then, in the late 1960s and early 1970s, things began to go wrong. The causes were partly external: in common with other industrial countries, Sweden suffered from the catastrophic rise in oil prices after the Arab-Israeli war of 1973. Shipbuilding was badly hit by falling world demand, and Sweden's excellent iron ore ran into strong competition from countries where it could be more cheaply produced. The main problems, however, were inherent to socialism, even of the Swedish variety. There was probably a theoretical time—let us say, for the sake of argument, around 1965—when the Social Democrats had got the mixture about right, for Sweden's needs and for the Swedish national character. But the trouble with legislators, especially socialist ones, is that they never know when to stop. The Swedish character itself had been profoundly marked by the decades of socialism. Expecting everything from the State, Swedish workers did not have much incentive to work, and Sweden developed the highest rate of industrial absenteeism in the world. Moreover, as is typical of socialist regimes, the bureaucracy kept on expanding. An astute Swedish political observer, Baron Carl von Platen, has described the process admirably in his book, *The Uneasy Truce* (Sherwood Press, 1983). As more and more married women took highly paid jobs, the mobility of Swedish labour was affected. As Platen put it: 'A husband does not want to move from, say, Stockholm to Malmö if his wife does not also get a good job in the new location.'

But the worst problem of all was the ever-expanding weight of taxes. As taxes increased, incentives for self-betterment decreased. Understandably many Swedes took to 'moonlighting,' creating a sizeable black economy. The same phenomenon has occurred in Britain and the United States, but in Sweden the disincentives of high taxation were considerably worse. By the time these lines were written the tax burden in Sweden had risen to 67 per cent of earned income.

The bureaucracy, as measured by the proportion of the country's gross domestic product (GDP) spent by the State, soared from less than 25 per cent in 1950 to more than 60 per cent in 1979. There are only about 8 million Swedes, yet more than 1.5 million of them work for the State in one form or another. To put it as simply as possible: Swedish socialism has almost strangled itself with its own bureaucracy.

This brings me back to my 'third Universal Rule of socialism': that it is incompatible with freedom. Of course, the Swedes are freer than, say, Soviet or Chinese citizens. But they are far less free than say, the British, Americans or French. With socialism the correlation is clear: the more socialism, the less freedom. Some years ago a basically sympathetic but honest and acute observer of Sweden, Roland Huntford of *The Observer*, wrote a powerful book which said it all in its title: *The New Totalitarians* (Stein & Day, New York, 1972). Huntford compares Swedish society with Aldous Huxley's hygienic nightmare of the 1930s, *Brave New World*. It would have been hard to prove that there was repression in Sweden or that human rights were violated. Certainly there were neither tortures nor concentration camps. But, as Huntford said, every detail of life was regulated by the bureaucracy, and by increasingly pervasive custom. It was morally unacceptable to the community that one should step out of line. In their 44 years of creeping socialism, the Swedes realised what Sidney and Beatrice Webb had only dreamed of in the Fabian Society—the 'inevitability of gradualness' had brought universal prosperity and welfare, at a high price in loss of liberty. And then, to complete the picture, the prosperity itself started to drain away.

THE USA: THE GREAT SOCIETY

The word 'socialism' does not readily occur to an outside observer of the United States. Yet the original home of the great unbridled capitalists of the early twentieth century—the Fords, the Rockefellers, and the Mellons—has by now absorbed a hefty dose of the stuff. It all began with the New Deal introduced by President Franklin D. Roosevelt after his election as the thirty-second president in 1932—at the height of the Great Depression. The New Deal involved a spate of legislation between 1933 and 1936 starting with agriculture and continuing with legislation affecting banking, home financing, gold and silver, relief for the unemployed, securities, labour and social security. Capitalism was to be tamed and wealth redistributed. The climax came with the Wealth Tax Act of August 1935 which invoked the federal power of taxation as a weapon against 'unjust concentration of wealth and economic power'. Increased surtaxes on individual yearly incomes of $50,000 and over were introduced.

Roosevelt was a Democrat, and ever since his Presidency welfarism in America has naturally been associated with Democratic administrations. This, however, is misleading. For example, it was the Republican President Dwight D. Eisenhower who launched the Department of Health, Education, and Welfare (popularly known as HEW) in 1953. True, it was the Democrat, President Lyndon B. Johnson, who legislated for his proposed Great Society in the 1960s, but it was under Republican Presidents Richard Nixon and Gerald Ford that the expansion of welfare really took off.

In May 1964 President Johnson, addressing a graduating class in Michigan, declared that 'in your time we have the opportunity to move not only toward the rich society and a powerful society, but upward to the Great Society'. In his *Memoirs* Richard Nixon was critical of Johnson's concept. The fatal flaw of the Great Society, he wrote, was 'its inclination to establish massive federal programs' (p. 267). In five years he recalls, Johnson's spending for the poor doubled, from $12.5 billion to $24.6 billion, while federal funds for health and education soared by over $18 billion.

In a powerful, brilliantly written book, *Wealth and Poverty* (Basic Books, New York, 1981), the American economist George Gilder lamented the consequences of what he called the 'actuarial State'. Unemployment compensation, he claimed, promotes unemployment: 'Aid for Families with Dependent Children (AFDC) makes more families dependent and fatherless. Disability insurance in all its multiple forms encourages the promotion of small ills into temporary disabilities and partial disabilities into total and permanent ones.' Gilder, whose book became a kind of Bible for the incoming Republicans under their new President, Ronald Reagan, goes on to record that during the 1970s 44 major welfare programmes grew two and a half times as fast as GNP and three times as fast as wages.

I am not sure that I go all the way with Gilder, impressive though his paean of praise for the moral values of capitalism undoubtedly is. He comes close to saying that *all* welfare is bad. I would stop short of so sweeping a condemnation. The problem, I believe, lies—in America as in Sweden and elsewhere—with knowing when to stop. The trouble is that the bureaucracies created by welfare feed on themselves and expand uncontrollably. If the end-result is national impoverishment, nobody benefits in the long term.

The Heritage Foundation in Washington, D.C., has issued some damning reports on the administration of welfare in the United States. In one of them, Jonathan R. Hobbs, under the title 'Welfare Need and Welfare Spending' (13 October 1982), exploded the popular myth that because defence spending was on the increase, welfare spending was necessarily decreasing. Indeed, defence spending *was* increasing: from $187.5 billion in financial year 1982 to $221.1 billion in 1983. But defence spending was clearly identifiable as such in its own specific budget. In contrast, welfare spending was disguised in the multiple budgets of 49 major national programmes (up from 44 under President Johnson). If all the items were added together, welfare expenditure for 1982 totalled $403.5 billion—more than twice the level of defence spending.

Hobbs is highly critical of the growth of welfare bureaucracy which had turned into an industry of more than 5 million public and private workers, to service 50 to 60 million recipients. The cost of welfare continued to soar and the net effect was to perpetuate poverty instead of abolishing it. Indeed Hobbs made an excellent case for abolishing 'poverty' while cutting welfare expenditure by up to 75 per cent. (The 'poverty threshold' had been defined by the Social Security Administration in 1964, based upon the amount spent by families of three or more on food.) The study ended with these words: 'When the United States is able to focus public assistance on the needs of the poor rather than on the expansionary interests of a government-controlled industry, Americans will save enormous sums of money, eliminate legions of bureaucrats and better serve the poor'.

Whether this view of welfare was a practical reality, and whether the Reagan administration would seriously set out to slash the welfare industry down to cost-effective proportions, remained to be seen when this book was written.

During Reagan's first term of office, it has to be said, the results were rather disappointing. In early 1985 the Heritage Foundation noted that the budget projection of 1985 of the Department of Health and Human Services (formerly HEW) stood at $322.1 billion—compared with $296 billion for 1984, and (to indicate the inexorable rise of inflation and the price of the services offered) actual expenditures of $112.4 billion in 1975.[3]

Re-elected in 1984 with a crushing majority, Reagan had proposed cuts of $167.9 billion for non-military expenditures, including the abolition of certain welfare programmes. The Senate however on 1 May

1984 voted in favour of restoring $22 billion for social security. Democracy, it seems, intrinsically favours socialism, or, to be more precise, it prevents the reform of egalitarianism in social security systems.

Even with a Reagan in power, in America as elsewhere, the cost of socialism remained exorbitant.

AFTER THE GERMAN MIRACLE

The example of the German Federal Republic (West Germany) is illuminating in ways that are subtly different from our other Western case studies. Everybody has heard of 'the German miracle', which the Germans call their *Wirtschaftswunder*. All that need be said about it here, as a reminder, is that out of the total destruction of World War Two, out of all the rubble and the misery, the economist Ludwig Erhard built an amazingly prosperous economy by sweeping away price and wage controls, abolishing rationing and allowing the market to rule. Erhard called his experiment a 'social market economy,' to show that he had not forgotten about the legitimate needs of welfare.

Thus under free enterprise and capitalism, defeated Germany (or rather the Western two-thirds of it) built the strongest economy in Western Europe, and (with Japan and the United States) one of the three strongest in the world.

It is often forgotten that this astonishing achievement persisted and improved on its own performance under the Grand Coalition which was in power in the Federal Republic from 1966 to 1969 when Willy Brandt and his Social Democrats took over.

The grandly-called Grand Coalition was so termed because it brought together West Germany's three main parties (or four, if you count the Christian parties separately): the Christian Democrats (CDU) and Christian Social Union (CSU); the Liberals (FDP); and the Social Democrats (SPD). Perhaps the most important aspect of the Grand Coalition was that the finance portfolio was in the hands of Franz-Josef Strauss, the Bavarian leader of the CSU. Interviewing Strauss at length for *Now!* magazine (15 February 1980), I asked him whether, in the event of his becoming Chancellor in the next elections, he would keep Erhard's 'social market economy' unchanged. His reply is worth quoting in full today, more than six years later:

> I would put it differently. I helped Erhard introduce the social market system as early as June 1948, against the votes of the communists and Helmut Schmidt's socialist friends. He was unable to dismantle it, but he inherited it from us.
>
> In fact, on his own past and even recent record, Mr Schmidt is an opponent of the system. The SPD wanted centralised economic planning and

advocated the so-called Deutschland Plan. If they had succeeded we would have had a confederation with the East German communists, with poverty and dependence on Moscow as the inevitable consequences.

Over the past ten years, the State sector of the economy has grown from 37 per cent to 47 per cent. During our twenty years in government (with myself as Finance Minister in Chancellor Kiesinger's Grand Coalition), our public debt totalled 14 billion DM for the whole period. During *each* of Helmut Schmidt's years in power the public debt grew by more than 150 per cent of our accumulated total. Today the debt is gigantic. I would not change the social market system, therefore: I would restore it to full efficiency.

But Strauss lost the elections in the spring of 1980. Schmidt and his Liberal friends came back. And the downward slide continued.

It would be unfair, perhaps, to rely entirely on the obviously interested verdict of Franz-Josef Strauss upon his rival Schmidt's socialist experiment. In fact the same picture, in far greater detail, is painted in the OECD's Economic Survey on *Germany* for 1981–82 (published in June 1982. Direct quotations follow (with key phrases italicised):

At the end of 1981, the public debt reached DM 545 billion, or 35 per cent of GNP . . . the authorities satisfied their financial requirements mainly in the form of loans against borrowing notes. . . .

Over the last twenty years the public sector has absorbed a *markedly increased share of total national output* and has been responsible for the redistribution of a greatly increased proportion of total national income. . . .

As far as the redistribution of income is concerned, the rapid growth of social security benefits and grants had added considerably to the growth of total household income *but has been outweighed by increases in direct taxes and social security contributions* with the overall result that transfers from the household to the government sector now represent about 18½ per cent of household disposable incomes, compared with just over 9 per cent at the beginning of the 1960s. Enterprises have been less affected by increases in direct taxes but have had to adjust to a large rise in employers' social security contributions which, as a proportion of operating surplus, have doubled from 15 per cent in 1960 to 30 per cent in 1980. [pp. 34–35]

In other words, the average family was drawing more in social security benefits than it used to do, but was paying out proportionately more than it got for the privilege. Welfare socialism, even of the comparatively mild West German variety, comes expensive. It is fair to ask, however, why the government should be charging the public more than it delivers in terms of education and health services (the main items involved). The OECD Survey gives part of the answer in my next quotation:

Although government has increased its value share of final expenditure on goods and services, a large part of this increase is attributable to *the faster*

*rise in the cost of providing public rather than private goods and services,
itself a function of the higher wage content of government activity . . . and its
lower growth in productivity.* [p. 37, emphasis added]

To be more precise, although the OECD Survey did not make the
point, the bureaucracy grows faster than the socialist benefits provided.
In fact between 1969 and 1980 the number of citizens whose livelihood
in one way or another depended on the State soared from 2.9 million to
4.4 million. To be honest, these figures are cited in a factual survey prepared by Verlag Information für die Wirtschaft ('Information of the
Economy' Publishers) in Bonn for the then main opposition party, the
Christian Democratic Union (CDU), in power from 1983 with its
Bavarian counterpart the Christian Social Union (CSU). But the figures
correspond with other relevant statistics in the OECD Survey, which,
for instance, records that between 1960 and 1980 government expenditure (expressed as a percentage of Gross Domestic Product) rose from
32 per cent to 47 per cent. Even the UK's government expenditure, during
the same period, rose 'only' to 45.5 per cent (from 32.6 per cent).

While government expenditure rose so did unemployment. From its
lowest point in 1965, when only 147,000 or 0.7 per cent of the labour
force were out of work, unemployment rose inexorably under Social
Democratic rule, reaching an estimated 2,350,000 or 9.5 per cent in
1983. I do not want to 'labour' this point, however, in the context of an
argument over the disadvantages of socialism. In the early 1980s, the
industrialised world as a whole was in the grip of deep recession. In
Britain, with Mrs Thatcher's Tory government in power, unemployment soared to well over 3 million. It would be wrong, therefore, to
attribute Germany's unemployment purely to the effect of socialism in
power—even if, as I believe, the underlying causes of Britain's bad performance certainly included the decades of trade union pressure for
wage increases unsupported by higher productivity.

Nor am I, as it may appear, against rising social welfare. Where
welfare socialism in advanced countries has gone off the rails is in the
insistence upon equal benefits for all regardless of need. This kind of
'equality' is a bottomless financial pit. Selective benefits for the really
needy—the old, the truly sick, the handicapped—could indeed be much
higher than they are in West Germany and elsewhere. And higher
benefits on a selective basis could well be met without incurring
massive, or indeed any, budgetary deficits. Unless a government can
meet the bills, without running up State expenditures and public debt,
however, welfare is a bad bargain for the voters. The Federal Republic
is by no means the worst example of welfare socialism in the West, but
the distortion caused by egalitarian doctrinalism is characteristic.

An acute observer of the German (and international) economic scene, Herbert Schmidt (a surviving pupil of the great Ludwig Erhard), recorded further facts and figures in *International Management into the 1990s*.[4] In a table on p. 17 Dr Schmidt recorded that the German public debt had risen by only 14 per cent from 1960 to 1970, but by 276 per cent from 1970 to 1980. As a percentage of GNP, the public debt stood at 17.2 per cent in 1960, at 18.5 per cent in 1970 and at 31 per cent ten years later. In 1980 federal debts alone for the first time exceeded the federal budget.

To this dangerous trend should be added the extraordinary readiness of the private banks in the Federal Republic to collect bad debts in the form of constantly 'rescheduled' loans to the Soviet-bloc countries, especially Poland. As I have pointed out elsewhere the West German banks are not alone in this folly, but they have indulged in it to an even greater extent than other banking systems.

The collapse of the coalition led by Helmut Schmidt and his Social Democrats in the autumn of 1982 and the subsequent sweeping victory of the Christian parties in the general elections of March 1983 may have rescued the Federal Republic from the impending consequences of socialism on the loose. Certainly the incoming government, under Helmut Kohl, had inherited a mess. The economic and financial picture emerging in mid-1986 was mixed. The OECD's report dated 17 July that year declared: 'More recently, employment has picked up markedly, but not sufficiently to bring unemployment down from its post-war record level.' In fact, unemployment stood at around 2.3 million. The 1987 budget, presented on 27 June 1986 by the Finance Minister, Dr Gerhard Stoltenberg, envisaged an increase of nearly 2.9 per cent in expenditure to DM 271,000 million. Public borrowing was also going up, though only slightly, from DM 23,700 million in 1986 to DM 24,300 million in 1987. Perhaps the time had come to resurrect Ludwig Erhard and move away from inherited socialism.

'PARTNERSHIP' IN AUSTRIA

Whenever the debate about socialism starts up, somebody is sure to raise a hand and ask, 'What about Austria, then? Long years of socialism, and the Austrians are doing very nicely, thank you.' Or words to that effect.

Let us then look at the Austrian example. The short answer to the kind of remark I have just quoted is that the socialists were in power in Austria for 13 years until Chancellor Bruno Kreisky fell in the 1983 elections, but the Austrian economic system could hardly be described as socialist. Alternatively, it was a rather peculiar, indeed unique, form of socialism.

The OECD Economic Survey of *Austria* (1982), gives a concise description of the Austrian system. After the Second World War, the Austrian Parliament decided *unanimously* to nationalise all the major sectors of the economy: the largest banks, the electricity companies, and most of the steel, mining, engineering and chemical industries. By the 1980s, the public sector employed about 30 per cent of the work force. Taking the 50 largest enterprises, however, the State-owned sector accounted for more than two-thirds of the total.

These facts alone might seem to qualify Austria for inclusion among the socialist States, at least by Western criteria. When it comes to *control* over the economy, however, the State turns out to be pretty feeble. It is not the government that determines economic policy, still less the elected Parliament. All economic policy decisions of importance are taken by the 'Social Partnership'—in practice, by a body known as the Paritätische Kommission (Parity Commission), a *privately* constituted body comprising equal representation of the trade unions, the employers' associations and the farmers' unions. The economic ministers do have a say, but strictly as junior partners.

To quote the OECD Survey: 'After the experience of civil war, political persecution and foreign occupation, political parties and social groups decided to bury their ideological differences and co-operate on a basis of equality, creating a political system that can be characterised as a parliamentary democracy with important *corporative* elements [p. 23, my emphasis].'

Wasn't it Mussolini who based his fascist State on the corporative principle? Does that mean Austria has a form of fascism? Let us not play with emotive words. The notion of 'corporations' representing economic and social interests was probably the one constructive idea in Mussolini's fascism. It may hurt some readers to admit it but the nearest equivalent to Austria's Parity Commission in recent European history was General Franco's 'vertical' trade unions (known as *sindicatos*), in which the employers as well as the workers were represented. The main difference—an important one—was that the Spanish *sindicatos* were in the last resort dominated by Franco's political organisation, known as the Movement, whereas the Austrian Parity Commission virtually excludes the government from decision-making.

In a perceptive article in *The Journal of Economic Affairs*, London, of January 1982, the Austrian economist Erich Streissler illustrated the point about governmental impotence in these words: 'to the amusement of the nation, he [Kreisky] has now found twice that he cannot even get rid of his Minister of Finance, Androsch, if the trade unions do not agree.'

This may seem like the kind of socialism Britain's still inordinately powerful unions like, but appearances are deceptive. Unlike Britain's trades unions, the Austrian unions practice wage restraint to an almost unbelievable degree. Professor Streissler records that in 1979 and 1980, at a time when the economy grew by 9 per cent, the President of the trade union federation, Anton Benya, decreed practically constant wages, and 'without creating unrest!'

Let Streissler give his verdict: 'The whole system can be called 'socialist' only by a heroic stretch of political imagination'.

So, yes, the Austrians did pretty well under a goverment of socialists. But they were *not* living under a socialist system. My universal rules of socialism therefore remain unaffected by the Austrian example.

NOTES

1 For a more detailed analysis of this left-wing takeover, see Brian Crozier, *The Minimum State* (Hamish Hamilton, 1979); see also Woodrow Wyatt, *What's Left of the Labour Party?* (Sidgwick & Jackson, 1977), and Stephen Haseler, *The Death of British Democracy* (Paul Elek, 1976).
2 *Op. cit.*, pp. 109–10.
3 Stuart M. Butler, Michael Sanera and W. Bruce Weinrod, *Mandate for Leadership II: Continuing the Conservative Revolution* (Washington DC, The Heritage Foundation, 1985), p. 91.
4 Edited by L. L. Waters for Indiana University; papers presented at an international conference, 27 September–1 October 1981.

11

EPILOGUE:
Disease and Cure

Fortunately for them, the philosophical dreamers of socialism are mostly dead, although new ones have emerged to take their places, undeterred by the universal failures of the socialist dream. The three Universal Rules stated in the Prologue survive intact from exposure to wide-ranging examples. Let us look again at our check-list of expectations:

(1) Common ownership. It was supposed to lead to greatly increased output. It has done nothing of the kind, except in the means of war.

(2) The distribution of wealth was to be fairer. Not in the USSR, where the ruling class does very well and the masses do miserably. Penal taxation of the better off in the intervals of Labour rule in Britain, to give another instance, may relieve the envious consciences of those in power but does less than nothing to help the poor.

(3) Class conflicts were to go. Instead, new elites are substituted for old. 'The New Class,' Djilas called it.

(4) Equal participation, said Lenin. Perhaps the biggest fraud of all.

(5) No more cyclical crises. Well, perhaps a point has to be conceded there: where permanent depression reigns, cycles are dormant.

(6) No racial or cultural distinctions. Try telling that to the Balts or the Uzbeks.

(7) No more wars. But look at Vietnam and Kampuchea.

THE ROOT OF EVIL

Certain further reflections are needed. If the great political evil of our times has been totalism under its diverse forms one is bound to recognise that their common origin, without exception, starts with socialism.

The defeat of Nazi Germany and fascist Italy played into the hands of Soviet propaganda, one of the objects of which is to poison Western public opinion by diverting its attention from the failure of the socialist experiment in the USSR. The hatred of the regimes of Hitler and Mussolini greatly attenuates criticism directed toward communism (the USSR having been the 'glorious ally' of the war years) and makes people forget the very real similarities between, for example, the Soviet Union and National Socialist Germany.

The historical reality remains that the ideas of the Utopian socialists, however attacked and even vilified by Karl Marx, are at the root of Marxism. They constitute the *primary source of totalism, of political evil.*

Moreover, socialism (including social democracy) serves as the antechamber of communism. Whatever may have been their original intentions, moderate socialists and social democrats are necessarily overtaken or outflanked by the forced bidding of Marxist–Leninists. Thus Kerensky yields to Lenin and, in our time, the Labour Party in Great Britain, which was deeply anti-communist in the days of Attlee and Gaitskell, is itself taken over by the extremists. In Federal Germany the 'moderate' Helmut Schmidt loses all control over his own Social Democratic Party (SPD).

But on the philosophical side, the origin of the ailment is even more fundamental than such examples might suggest. The dreamers of socialism, indignant before the injustice and inequality of the human condition, offer total 'solutions' by which they believe they can transform the world. The communities of Robert Owen and the *phalanstères* of Charles Fourier could easily have transformed themselves into totalist regimes had it not been for the absence of the means of power, the means of mass communication, which did not exist at that time. These means Lenin, Mussolini, Hitler and Stalin had: hence totalism.

As Milovan Djilas, the Yugoslav dissident, has justly observed, Karl Marx was no less 'Utopian' than the philosophers whose Utopianism he denounced. But unlike the others he had understood the necessity to seize power. Utopia, plus power, becomes totalism.

THE REMEDY—THE MINIMUM STATE

All our governments are more or less strongly dosed with socialism. All our people suffer from it. The proliferation of bureaucracies, the interference of the State in industry and even in commerce, weigh down national budgets, to the great loss of consumers and taxpayers. The political class even in that section which claims to be 'liberal' (or 'conservative' according to the country and the language), benefits from it and hesitates to undertake the necessary reforms even when their necessity is grasped. Moreover, certain sectors of society, notably the trades unions (especially in Great Britain), are deeply attached to socialist ideas, in which they find the basis of their own power. In fact these ideas are the basis of political strikes.

What is to be done? The well-known ex-Communist French writer Jean-François Revel said in his book *How Democracies Finish* that democracies are in danger of dying because they have lost the will to defend themselves against Soviet imperialism. I do not contest this judgement but this is only one aspect of the sickness of democracies; they also run the risk of dying because they are suffocated by socialism. Governments neglect the central reasons for their own existence to the benefit of relatively less important sectors. It is imperative to push back the frontiers of the State: this is a condition of survival for democracies. It is necessary to take care, however. One needs to know where to reduce and where to preserve, where even to strengthen the indispensable sectors that tend to be neglected because of the prevailing search for socialism. What are these indispensable sectors? There is no mystery about them. They concern the basic points which alone justify the existence of the State:

(1) Internal security: the protection of citizens against crime; the security of the State in the face of subversion and espionage; the maintenance of public order, etc.
(2) Defence of the State against its external enemies.
(3) The maintenance of the value of money.

With the sole exception of Switzerland I cannot think of any example in the whole world of a democracy where these three conditions are fulfilled: one of the three, possibly, or two of the three, but never all three at the same time. And yet our governments devote enormous sums to relatively less important tasks that fall within the purview of the State.

THE GUILT OF THE PARTIES

General de Gaulle had taken note of the failure of political parties in power or in opposition during the Fourth Republic. He wanted his Rally of the French People to become an organisation whose role would be above political parties. He failed, although by increasing the authority of the Head of State in the constitution of the Fifth Republic he did succeed in reducing to that extent the capacity of the parties to impair the working of the State.

Are political parties in fact an indispensable element of democracy? It is worth putting the question.

An 'achievable Utopia' would consist of creating a political organism (which might be styled a 'political college') that would ensure the good management of the State while preserving individual liberties and the essential principles of the democracy (the alternation of groups in power and the right of voters to change their government by the peaceful use of the polling booths), on the basis of the following principles:

(1) Two candidates to contest all parliamentary seats, thus giving voters a choice between the personal qualities of the candidates rather than the rival programmes of adversarial political parties.

(2) Losers as well as winners to enter the elected assembly; the winners to constitute the governing group and the losers the opposition for the duration of the parliament.

(3) Each candidate to be forbidden to present himself or herself for re-election in the same constituency at forthcoming elections, thus causing an automatic change in the governing group and a mathematical guarantee of alternation.

In previous books, but especially in *The Minimum State* (Hamish Hamilton, 1979), I considered the possibilities of such a system in exhaustive detail. I shall not go over the same ground here. One point, however, needs to be restated. It is temptingly easy to assume that representative democracy is here to stay. In fact, it is a fragile and vulnerable system and historically very recent. Moreover, it is riddled with inconsistencies and flaws. It is worth the effort, therefore, to consider the imperfections soberly and to inquire whether and to what extent it is possible to preserve the undoubted benefits of such systems while reducing the imperfections.

One thing is evident: a system such as I have outlined above could be created only on the basis of a constitution that would guarantee the essential principles of the State, while limiting State participation in the economy of the country. To put it another way: democracy will not survive wherever the dose of socialism becomes incompatible with the survival of freedom.

Index